A HOUND DOG TALE

A HOUND DOG TALE

and the SONG THAT CHANGED EVERYTHING

Ben Wynne

LOUISIANA STATE UNIVERSITY PRESS
BATON ROUGE

Published with the assistance of the V. Ray Cardozier Fund

Published by Louisiana State University Press
lsupress.org

Manufactured in the United States of America
Second printing, 2025

DESIGNER: Michelle A. Neustrom
TYPEFACE: Minion Pro
PRINTER AND BINDER: Sheridan Books, Inc.

JACKET PHOTOGRAPHS: Willie Mae "Big Mama" Thornton (*top*), courtesy Ralston Crawford Collection of Jazz Photography, Hogan Archive of New Orleans Music and New Orleans Jazz, Tulane University Special Collections; and Elvis Presley (*bottom*) featured in *TV Radio Mirror* magazine, September 1956.

LIBRARY OF CONGRESS CATALOGING-IN-PUBLICATION DATA

Names: Wynne, Ben, 1961– author.
Title: A hound dog tale : Big Mama, Elvis, and the song that changed everything / Ben Wynne.
Description: Baton Rouge : Louisiana State University Press, 2024. | Includes bibliographical references and index.
Identifiers: LCCN 2023024673 (print) | LCCN 2023024674 (ebook) | ISBN 978-0-8071-8114-0 (cloth) | ISBN 978-0-8071-8150-8 (pdf) | ISBN 978-0-8071-8149-2 (epub)
Subjects: LCSH: Rock music—United States—1951–1960—History and criticism. | Blues (Music)—1951–1960—History and criticism. | Stoller, Mike. Hound dog. | Music and race—United States—History—20th century. | Presley, Elvis, 1935–1977. | Stoller, Mike. | Leiber, Jerry. | Thornton, Big Mama.
Classification: LCC ML3534.3 .W96 2024 (print) | LCC ML3534.3 (ebook) | DDC 782.42166—dc23/eng/20230621
LC record available at https://lccn.loc.gov/2023024673
LC ebook record available at https://lccn.loc.gov/2023024674

for my family

Contents

Illustrations

Acknowledgments

I could not have produced this work without the assistance of many people. As always, Rand Dotson and the staff at LSU Press have been extremely helpful and easy to work with, and I owe them a great debt. Thanks also to Neal Novak, and to Derik Shelor, whose editing talents certainly enhanced the manuscript. The research for this book could not have been completed without the assistance of the staffs from a number of archives and libraries, including the John Harrison Hosch Library at the University of North Georgia, Gainesville, Georgia; the Center for Popular Music at Middle Tennessee State University, Murfreesboro, Tennessee; the Mississippi Department of Archives and History, Jackson, Mississippi; the J. D. Williams Library at the University of Mississippi, the Tennessee State Library and Archives, Nashville, Tennessee; the Alabama Department of Archives and History, Montgomery, Alabama; the Georgia Department of Archives and History, Atlanta, Georgia; the Southern Historical Collection at the University of North Carolina, Chapel Hill, North Carolina; the Texas State Historical Association, Austin, Texas; the Robert W. Woodruff Library at Emory University, Atlanta, Georgia; the Rock and Roll Hall of Fame, Cleveland, Ohio; the Ned R. McWherter Library, University of Memphis, Memphis, Tennessee; the Archives of African American Music and Culture, Indiana University, Bloomington, Indiana; the Country Music Hall of Fame, Nashville, Tennessee; the Library of Congress and National Archives in Washington, D.C.; the Cook Library at the University of Southern Mississippi, Hattiesburg, Mississippi; and the Millsaps-Wilson Library at Millsaps College, Jackson, Mississippi. At one time or another I have benefitted from the counsel or example of a number of former professors and colleagues, and I would like to thank them as well. They include Charles Sallis, Robert McElvaine, Ron Howard, Kirk Ford, Robert Haws, David Sansing, Ted Ownby, Nancy Bercaw, Charles Reagan Wilson, Sheila Skemp, Michael Namorato, Charles Eagles, James C. Cobb, and W. Scott Poole. I would also like to acknowledge every teacher that I had at St. Andrew's Episcopal School in Jackson, Mississippi, from the first grade in 1967 through my senior year in 1979. They laid the foundation for my life at what I believe is one of the best schools in the nation.

I am fortunate to work at the University of North Georgia in Gainesville, Georgia, where the administration at every level is supportive of my teaching and publishing pursuits. Along with many other members of our university community, I have benefitted from the generosity of our former president Bonita Jacobs, who was always quick to provide encouragement and resources for all types of scholarly activity. I also owe a great debt of gratitude to Chaudron Gille, Provost; Chris Jespersen, Dean of the College of Arts and Letters; Ric Kabat and Tim May, Associate Deans of the College of Arts and Letters; Jeff Pardue, Department Head for the History, Anthropology, and Philosophy Department; and Tamara Spike, Associate Department Head for the History, Anthropology, and Philosophy Department, all of whom help keep our corner of the university on a positive course. I would also like to recognize my colleagues in the History, Anthropology and Philosophy Department, who foster a warm and collegial work atmosphere conducive to academic ventures of all kinds. I could not work with a better group. Friends John Leggett, Marty Lester, Alan Vestal, Charles G. Sallis, Bill Hetrick, Brant Helvenston, Ted Moise, Doug Walker, Johnny Greer, Philip Gaines, Eric Stracener, Robin Rushing, Lynn Ashford, Richard Nolen, Fred Duggan, Bill Fisher, Chuck McIntosh, and Necip Alican all contributed to this effort directly or in spirit. Last but certainly not least, nothing I do is possible without the support and love of my family, Carly, Lily, Cotton, Patricia, and Noelle. They keep me going, and I dedicate this book to them.

A HOUND DOG TALE

INTRODUCTION

[Rock 'n' roll] smells phony and false. It is sung, played, and written for the most part by cretinous goons.

—**FRANK SINATRA,** quoted in James Kaplan, *Sinatra: The Chairman*

I admire the man. He's a great success and a fine actor, but I think he shouldn't have said it. He was mistaken about that.

—**ELVIS PRESLEY,** *Nashville (Tenn.) Banner,* October 29, 1957

On the evening of June 5, 1956, Elvis Presley walked onto a soundstage in Los Angeles and altered American popular culture forever. He was appearing on a national television program that was named for and hosted by former vaudeville and radio comedian Milton Berle. Berle did not understand Presley's music, but he knew about television ratings, and from that standpoint he recognized that the singer's appearance on his program was significant. As for Presley, the singer was already popular with teenagers, but he was not yet the phenomenon that he would become. His appearance on *The Milton Berle Show* was supposed to be just another step along the singer's path as a rising star, but it turned out to be much more than that. On the program, Presley sang a song titled "Hound Dog," which he had been using in his stage act but had not yet recorded. His animated interpretation of the tune thrilled teenagers across the United States as it bewildered and outraged many older viewers. The next day, newspaper all over the country reported what Presley had done, setting in motion a chain of events that greatly accelerated his rise to the status of global icon. "Hound Dog" became the singer's signature tune to the point that over time the song's title and Presley's name became almost synonymous. Ironically, as “Hound Dog” helped Presley make history on Berle’s program, most viewers were unaware that the song had a powerful history of its own. Before “Hound Dog” ever reached Presley, it had a past filled with high drama and a host of artistically colorful and occasionally dangerous personalities.

When first conceived and recorded, the rock ’n’ roll classic “Hound Dog” gave little indication of its potential power. It was a good song that was catchy but not extraordinary, a coarse, grinding blues with the ancient but familiar theme of conflict between a woman and a man. At the time, no one recognized it as the product of a unique synthesis of race and cultures, and certainly no one knew that it was destined to become one of the most explosive and instantly recognizable entries in the American songbook. Most of the many recorded versions of “Hound Dog” that exist today are no more than three minutes long, but the song is the product of a backstory that is lengthy, complicated, and peppered with a broad, eclectic cast of characters. First, there were the two white, Jewish teenagers, one from New York and the other from Baltimore, who wanted to be Black and ended up becoming one of the most celebrated songwriting teams of all time. Then there was the three-hundred-pound African American woman, a blues belter from Alabama, whose infectious primal growl demanded the immediate attention and respect of anyone within earshot. She could dominate a room, startling and captivating audiences in equal measure. A Las Vegas bandleader, originally from Philadelphia, played an unlikely but essential role in eventually bringing “Hound Dog” to the masses, though not with his own group. And of course, there was the impoverished white boy from rural Mississippi who rose to become the most famous entertainer in the world. They were all part of the story, as were a host of record executives, producers, musicians, and arrangers. They all made “Hound Dog” what it became, not just a song, but a multigenerational, multicultural rock ’n’ roll masterpiece.

This book traces the complicated development of a simple song, beginning with the songwriters, Jerry Leiber and Mike Stoller, two white teenagers obsessed with Black culture. While they were expert musical craftsmen, neither seemed to fully accept the hard truth that they could never be Black, no matter how hard they tried. They used language that they perceived to be Black, which to them meant cool, and wrote music for African American artists. One of those was Willie Mae "Big Mama" Thornton, who recorded their hit song "Hound Dog" in 1953. Leiber, Stoller, and Thornton crossed paths through two other significant figures in the "Hound Dog" story, Johnny Otis and Don Robey. Otis was a musician, bandleader, arranger, and one of the giants of rhythm and blues on the West Coast, while "Diamond Don" Robey was a sometimes violent producer, label owner, and nightclub impresario with reputed ties to organized crime. Thornton caught Robey's attention when she sang in one of his clubs, after which he approached Otis to find something for her to record. At Otis's request, Leiber and Stoller wrote "Hound Dog," which was a huge hit, ending up #1 on the *Billboard* R&B charts.

Once Thornton's song became a hit, a host of cover versions, answer songs, and unauthorized copies by other artists followed, crossing the color line from rhythm and blues to country music, and then back again. Most of the R&B versions were straight copies of the original, while country renderings usually featured steel guitars and singers with an unmistakable hillbilly twang. One of the most notable copies came out of a tiny studio in Memphis owned by Sam Phillips. Phillips, who was yet to become famous for his association with Elvis Presley, Jerry Lee Lewis, and Johnny Cash, altered the words to "Hound Dog," changed the title to "Bear Cat," and recorded it with Memphis disc jockey Rufus Thomas singing lead. That record would have probably been just another forgettable derivative of the original had Phillips not decided to take sole writing credit for the song. The move generated a lawsuit filed by Robey, who had the publishing rights to "Hound Dog." Phillips lost the suit, which at the time represented a significant setback for his fledgling label, Sun Records.

The invisible man in the "Hound Dog" story has always been Las Vegas lounge singer Freddie Bell. A Philadelphia native, Bell led a group called Freddie Bell and the Bellboys, who enthusiastically covered the latest hits, including tamer versions of notable blues, R&B, and rock 'n' roll records. After relocating to Las Vegas, they added "Hound Dog" to their stage act, but in a manner that altered the song's timing and the gritty spirit of the original. Bell changed or "cleaned up" many of the words to fit his Vegas sensibilities, and he and the band performed the song as a novelty number. They had a steady gig in the lounge at the Sands Hotel, where one night they ran into Elvis Presley. Presley was making his first appearance in Las Vegas, and on a night off he and his band were sampling the city's nightlife. They caught Freddie Bell and the Bellboys' act at the Sands, and the event changed music history. Presley liked the way that Freddie Bell did "Hound Dog," and decided to add the song to his own act. This set in motion a chain of events that eventually made "Hound Dog" a global phenomenon.

Presley took the song and ran with it. He used Bell's lyrics onstage, but the force of his personal charisma turned "Hound Dog" into a huge hit, even with the sanitized words. Most nights he closed his show with it, and he sang it during three legendary television appearances. The first was on the *Milton Berle Show,* where the sexually suggestive bumps and grinds included in his performance scandalized a large segment of the country, and made him even more popular with teenagers. Next came the *Steve Allen Show,* where the host tried to subdue—and some said humiliate—Presley by forcing him to dress in a tuxedo and sing "Hound Dog" to an actual basset hound. Finally, Presley performed the song during each of his three appearances on the *Ed Sullivan Show.* The appearances with Sullivan pushed Presley's career to even greater heights, and were a catalyst for the transition of rock 'n' roll into the American cultural mainstream. Afterward, "Hound Dog" became one of the most covered rock 'n' roll songs in history, with hundreds of artists recording their own versions, and still more including it in their stage acts.

The 1956 release of Presley's "Hound Dog" also marked a line of demarcation. He was already popular, but the song hastened the process of the young singer becoming a truly unstoppable force. It was a clear, unmistakable signal to an older generation that a new youth culture was emerging in America, and they were powerless to stop it. The song was a three-minute testament to everything that American elders hated or feared about rock 'n' roll. It was wild and loud, and the words made no sense to the older folks. Worse than that, it was sexually suggestive, and the effect that it had on teenagers was uncontrollable. Like rock 'n' roll itself, the song was the product of a type of racial interaction that unnerved many American whites. It blurred the lines between white and Black culture in a way that some viewed as dangerous, and it would later spur discussion about cultural appropriation. In that context, the song's first line, "You ain't nothin' but a hound dog," was not just a signature lyric. It was a battle cry.

Chapter 1

The SONGWRITERS

We wanted to be black.
We loved that music culture.

—**MIKE STOLLER,** *Chicago Tribune,* June 12, 1994

If there was a specific date when the "Hound Dog" story began, it might be March 13, 1933, the day that Michael "Mike" Stoller was born in the Bell Harbor neighborhood of Queens, New York. Stoller was a third-generation Jewish American. His father, Abraham, worked long hours as a structural engineer and draftsman, and his grandfather Louis was a Russian immigrant who, according to census records, came to the United States around the turn of the twentieth century. If Mike Stoller's artistic proclivities were the product of genetics, they may have come from his mother's side of the family. Adelyn Endore was born in Pittsburgh, the daughter of an Austrian immigrant. By the 1920s, her family was living in New York City, where she married Abraham Stoller at the municipal chapel in 1928. Before the couple wed, Adelyn was a model and actress who appeared on Broadway and briefly dated the composer George Gershwin. Her brother, Guy, was a prolific novelist and screenwriter who was later blacklisted during the Red Scare of the 1950s, and her sister, Celia, was an accomplished concert pianist who gave music lessons to help make ends meet. "They lived right near the Gershwins, and they were friendly," Stoller later told an interviewer when asked about his mother's people. "She knew Ira [Gershwin] also and she went to school with Frankie, who was the sister, Frances Gershwin."[1]

Young Mike Stoller's introduction to the world of playing music was a bit rocky. At age five he took piano lessons from his aunt, but she was a stern taskmaster, quick to rap the youngster's knuckles if he hit a sour note. He quit after a few lessons but maintained a love for music that eventually translated into professional success. While Stoller would one day be famous for writing hit pop and rock tunes, WQXR, a New York radio station that specialized in classical compositions, was one of the foundational musical influences of his early life. With origins dating back to 1929, the station was a mainstay of highbrow broadcasting in the city. It boasted that listeners could "tune in at breakfast time to Mozart, listen to Beethoven after dinner, retrace the movements of a beloved concerto before bedtime, [and] familiarize one's self with modem music on a Sunday evening, or with an opera rarely heard, on Sunday afternoon." Stoller's mother tuned in to the station every day. "The sun came out, and WQXR, the classical station, played continually," Stoller later wrote. "I grew up on Strauss, Shostakovich, and Sibelius."[2]

There were other influences as well, some of which were far more mysterious and exciting to a teenager than the classical offerings on the radio. Not long after he stopped taking lessons from his aunt, Stoller moved with his family to the Sunnyside neighborhood in Queens, where he took an interest in Black culture, and particularly Black music. His parents sent him to an integrated summer camp, where he mixed with African Americans and observed elements of their culture firsthand. "It was an interracial summer camp in New Jersey, near Hackettstown," he said. "It was totally interracial, the counselors as well as the kids. I heard a Black teenager playing boogie-woogie piano in the barn, which was our recreation hall. . . . I was mesmerized."[3]

His life forever altered, Stoller signed on for more piano lessons. He studied with a neighborhood teacher, but classical fare paled in comparison to the intoxicating rhythms that he discovered at camp. Through a stroke of luck, he was also able to take a few lessons from James P. Johnson, one of the most popular jazz pianists of the 1920s. Called by some the "King of Jazz" in New York, Johnson mentored a number of younger musicians who later had significant careers, including Thomas Wright "Fats" Waller. One of Stoller's neighbors knew Johnson and, after hearing the youngster play, made the necessary introductions. Johnson was past his prime when Stoller met him, but he was willing to give the boy a few lessons, which was enough to make a lasting impression. He taught Stoller "the structure of blues and boogie-woogie . . . the knowledge of the 12-bar structure," which served Stoller well in the future as he started writing songs.[4]

In addition to hearing boogie-woogie piano at his summer camp, Stoller also met Al Levitt there. Levitt, who would grow up to be an accomplished jazz drummer, became Stoller's friend and musical co-conspirator. Levitt lived in Manhattan, and Stoller visited him frequently. As teenagers, the two boys covered a lot of ground, hitting the streets on a regular basis in search of live jazz and blues. The boys usually made a beeline for 52nd Street—specifically the block between Fifth and Sixth Avenues—where music spilled out into the streets from innumerable jazz clubs. "Swing Street," as the area was known internationally, routinely hosted the world's best jazz artists in venues like the Onyx, the Famous Door, Jimmy Ryan's, the Downbeat, Hickory House, Kelly's Stable, and the Three Deuces. "We loved Fats Waller and Count Basie and modern mainstreamers like Coleman Hawkins and Lester Young," Stoller later remembered in his autobiography. "But most exciting of all was the scene at the Three Deuces, one of the main Fifty-Second Street clubs, where Charlie 'Yardbird' Parker was in charge. Bird was the resident genius of Fifty-Second Street." The underage boys snuck into all the clubs, as well as a major concert at Carnegie Hall featuring Dizzy Gillespie, Parker, and Ella Fitzgerald.[5]

As Stoller frequented the jazz clubs, his interest in African American music and culture grew exponentially. In addition to their forays to Swing Street, he and Levitt made almost weekly trips to Harlem, where, through one of their camp counselors, they joined a private social club headquartered in a multistory building on 125th Street. There they shot pool and mingled with an army of amateur musicians with big dreams of one day making a name for themselves. Back at home, Stoller's relaxed racial attitudes raised eyebrows in his neighborhood, especially after he escorted an African American girl to the junior prom at his virtually all-white Forest Hills High School. "I created something of a scandal," he said. "Forest Hills wasn't ready for interracial dating. I was."[6]

Stoller and Levitt ran around together for two or three years, until Stoller's father decided to pack up and move the family to Los Angeles. The elder Stoller was looking for better business opportunities that never quite materialized, but his son flourished in the new environment. In California, Mike

Stoller attended Belmont High School, where the student body was heavily Hispanic and African American. He broadened his musical knowledge base by joining the Vasquez Brothers Band, a group that played jazz, along with "some Latino numbers." They played regularly at the Alexandria Hotel in downtown Los Angeles, where Chet Baker occasionally sat in on trumpet. Stoller's bandmates taught him a great deal about traditional Mexican music. Around the same time, Stoller studied arranging with Arthur Lange. Lange was the conductor of the Santa Monica Orchestra and a successful film score composer. "I was into all kinds of music," Stoller said, "Arthur Lange was teaching me to write for a symphony orchestra, [and] the Vasquez Brothers were teaching me *rancheras.*" In the midst of all this activity, Stoller finished his last year of high school in 1950 and enrolled in Los Angeles City College. Not long afterward, he met Jerry Leiber, the man with whom he would alter the history of popular music.[7]

Jerome "Jerry" Leiber was born in Baltimore, Maryland, on April 25, 1933, six weeks after Mike Stoller was born in New York. He was the son of Jacob and Manya Leiber, Jewish immigrants who came to the United States from Poland in 1921. The family—including Jerry's two older sisters—lived in a modest home at 1235 Hollins Street and owned a grocery store next door. "Until I went to kindergarten I spoke broken English," Leiber, recalled. "I spoke a combination of Yiddish and street English that I picked up from the streets and my mother, my family. I didn't really learn how to speak [proper] English until I went to the kindergarten." The family mixed with other immigrants, and among the boy's earliest musical memories were Polish folk tunes played at neighborhood parties that he attended with his mother. Leiber was also born with a genetic quirk that gave him one brown eye and one blue, which made him a somewhat memorable character to everyone he met.[8]

Tragedy struck the household in 1939 when Leiber's father died of a cerebral hemorrhage at age forty-two. To make matters worse, he died on his son Jerry's sixth birthday. The family was traumatized, but afterward Manya Leiber kept the store afloat. She eventually sold the Hollins Street business and bought another store that sold groceries as well as "pots and pans and everything in between" on the corner of Riggs and McKean Avenues, near several predominantly Black neighborhoods. Her nine-year-old son ran errands and made deliveries in the area, which brought him into contact

Songwriters Mike Stoller (*left*) and Jerry Leiber (*right*) penned "Hound Dog" for Willie Mae "Big Mama" Thornton. David Attie/Getty Images.

with many African Americans. For Jerry, the experience was transformative. "I was very much involved in what was going on down there," he later remembered.[9]

While there was racial friction in the area, the Leibers got along well with most of the African Americans that they dealt with. "My mother was the only grocery store in a radius of maybe three or four miles that extended credit to black people. Nobody else did," Jerry later remembered. "So I was a welcomed character in the neighborhood, in the black neighborhood." Leiber made deliveries for several years, during which time he immersed himself in African American culture. He hung out with local Black kids, heard their street corner banter, ate in their homes, and listened to their music. Because his own neighborhood was rough on Jews, particularly those who seemed comfortable around African Americans, he later claimed that he could relate to his Black friends as an oppressed minority. Although he did not think much about it at the time, he later told an interviewer that his years delivering staples to African American homes probably sparked his early interest in Black music and laid the foundation for his future songwriting success. "I think it was in my head," he said. "You know, I was always there playing on the street, in their houses, hearing things. I think it became second nature to me. In fact, to some degree, I think I imitated Black cultural attitudes and styles as a child for so long that it became second nature to me."[10]

Leiber's interest in African American culture did not sit well with some whites in his neighborhood, who called him names and leveled threats. His affinity for Black music also caused some trouble at home. Leiber had an uncle who owned the only piano in the family, and made his house available for the boy to take piano lessons from a local instructor. All went well until the uncle arrived home unexpectedly one day and heard his nephew tinkering with blues and boogie-woogie chord progressions. He gave Leiber an ultimatum: stop playing that type of music or stop playing the piano at his house. For the youngster there was no choice. As a result of the altercation, Leiber abruptly quit playing piano altogether and took up the drums. He took lessons at Fred Walker's music store, Baltimore's leading music emporium. Walker's was housed in a large, two-story building on Howard Street, with the bottom floor reserved for records and sheet music, and the top floor dedicated to instruments. Leiber did not have a set of drums at home, but he befriended another kid who owned "a set of white pearl Gretsch drums that absolutely floored me." His friend let him use the set at his house after school. With limited practice time, Leiber could only learn so much as a performer, but through it all he maintained his musical focus on blues and jazz.[11]

By 1945, Leiber's two older sisters, Helen and Lillian, had escaped their Baltimore environs and relocated to the West Coast. Lillian enrolled at the University of California at Berkeley, and Helen was about to marry a chief petty officer in the navy. Their mother wanted to be closer to them, so she sold her store and, along with Jerry, boarded a bus for the 2,600-mile journey to a new home in Los Angeles. "The next thing I knew we were on a Greyhound bus heading west," Leiber later said. "It was late summer, and the ride was endless." Leiber and his mother arrived in California just in time to celebrate the end of the Second World War. They moved into a small bungalow in the Larchmont neighborhood, not far from Paramount Studios in Hollywood. While it represented a departure from almost everything he had known up to that point, Leiber made a smooth transition to the West Coast. "I loved California," he said. "The palm trees, the movie stars. I didn't see one movie star, but I knew they were there." The boy took drama classes at John Burrows Junior High School and, like many kids in the area, developed vague ambitions related to acting. Along those lines, he got a summer job at a local theater. It was not complicated work. He sold tickets and soft drinks, helped patrons to their seats, and swept up as he fantasized about a show business career.[12]

Fortunately for generations of popular music lovers, Leiber's dreams of becoming an actor never panned out. He spent two years doing odd jobs at the theater before throwing in the towel, but a new opportunity soon presented itself. As fate would have it, the petty officer that Leiber's sister Helen married happened to be Franklyn Tableporter. He was the son of Lewis Tableporter, a New York transplant to Los Angeles who had shortened his surname to Porter and established himself as a songwriter who also scored films. The elder Porter took a shine to Leiber and placed him securely under his wing. "I became sort of a pet of Lew Porter," Leiber said. "Lew used to take me in his car to the different studios where he was working, and I loved it. I went around with him and got the [songwriting] bug. I liked the environment. It was exciting."[13]

Leiber attended Fairfax High School, where few of his white classmates listened to Black music. While he had friends, he was more of a loner than an outcast in that regard. His musical education continued when he got a part-time job in a restaurant where an African American cook kept the kitchen radio tuned to his favorite stations. "I was listening to the black stations, the blues stations primarily, sometimes the jazz stations, but primarily the black blues stations," Leiber remembered. "I loved the records that I heard. I'd hear things like Jimmy Witherspoon singing 'Ain't Nobody's Business,' and stuff by Amos Milburn and Memphis Slim." One of Leiber's favorite radio programs was *Harlematinee,* hosted by Hunter Hancock on KFVD. Hancock was a native Texan who some credit as being the first white disc jockey on the West Coast to play rhythm and blues records. His one-hour program promised "from bebop to ballad, swing to sweet, the blues to boogie . . . some of the very best in rhythm and blues records, featuring some of the greatest and most popular Negro singers, musicians, and entertainers in the world." Leiber listened intently.[14]

By the time he was fifteen, Leiber was filling notebooks with song lyrics, most of which sprang from his love of African American culture. He focused primarily on the blues, with little patience for other styles. He listened to jazz, but only in passing, and he had no interest in country music or the typical pop fare of the era. His lyrics were based on his observations of the Black community and his perceptions of the manner in which that community functioned. "I was only interested in the language and the humor and the pain, whatever, of the blues," he said. It was an odd dynamic. A white Jewish teenager from Baltimore who believed he could write in the African American vernacular, seemingly unaffected by the great truth that no matter what he did, he could never be Black and comment on life from an African American perspective.[15]

The next step in Leiber's journey was to try to look the part. He slowly altered his wardrobe until he became "a bit of a dandy, a bit of a hipster. A bit of this and a bit of that." He got a new job at Norty's Music Center, an eclectic record shop on Fairfax Avenue owned by Norty Beckman. The store featured "dependable Jewish standards" on one wall, "contemporary pop" on the other, and also carried blues records. Leiber served as shipping clerk and counter man, which meant that, in addition to dealing with customers, he met record salesmen and a few executives who wanted the store to stock their music. He did not make any direct decisions on purchases, but he did get to hobnob. Much of what the store sold was benign pop fare that could never match the blues, but for a self-described "impassioned would-be songwriter" the job was one step closer to show business. "I worked there to be closer to the music," Leiber later said.[16]

Among the people who Leiber met while working at Norty's was Lester Sill, who would become a mentor. Born in Philadelphia in 1918, Sill had come west after military service during the Second World War. He and his brother-in-law opened a nightclub at 35th and Western Avenue called Cotton's Club. It was an after-hours joint that employed many Black acts as entertainment. Not long afterward, Sill struck up a friendship with Lester Bihari, who lived in his building. Lester and his brothers, Julius, Saul, and Joseph, founded Modern Records, one of the labels that was influential in spreading rhythm and blues music to the West Coast. Modern put out John Lee Hooker's "Boogie Chillen" in 1948 and later worked with Bobby "Blue" Bland, Jimmy Witherspoon, Etta James, and Ike and Tina Turner among others. Sill went to work for the company as a salesman and made the rounds constantly in a territory stretching from Fresno to San Diego, including Los Angeles. "It was really fantastic," he later said. "And I got into working in the studio with Julius [Bihari] producing. I would work with Witherspoon, B. B. King, Hadda Brooks, Pee Wee Crayton. Those kinds of people." During his travels around California, Sill stopped at record outlets, radio stations, café's with jukeboxes, and innumerable African American mom and pop stores that included records with the general merchandise or groceries that they sold. One of the places Sill stopped on a regular basis was Norty's, where he met Jerry Leiber.[17]

In *Hound Dog: The Leiber and Stoller Autobiography* (2009), Leiber said that Sill came into Norty's one day wearing an expensive suit and carrying an armful of records. In full salesman mode, he played some of the sides for the young clerk, even though Leiber had no authority to make purchases for the store. One of the songs Sill played was Hooker's "Boogie Chillen." "Lester Sill brought in this new epiphany," Leiber said. "He embodied it. He was wearing a tan, double-breasted suit with a subtle powder blue pinstripe. His suit mightily impressed me. But 'Boogie Chillen' impressed me even more." Modern's releases were just the sort of music that Leiber had become obsessed with back in Baltimore. After playing the records, Sill fell into casual conversation with the clerk, asking him what he wanted to do for a living. Leiber said that he wanted to be a songwriter, and that he had already written a few songs. Sill was interested in some of Leiber's lyrics, but wanted to see the music that went along with them. When Leiber told the record salesman that he did not write music, Sill supposedly told him to "find somebody who does." As the story goes, Sill's words led Leiber to search out a musical partner, Jerry Horowitz, a local drummer who also had an interest in writing. The two got along, but the partnership did not work out. Horowitz's father passed away and he had to quit music in search of a steadier paycheck.

Before he left, he suggested that Leiber get in touch with a pianist that he knew, which turned out to be Mike Stoller. "[Horowitz] told me that he had a musician's name written down who was a piano player that he played a dance with," Leiber recalled. "And that he might be interested in writing songs. He wrote his number down and gave it to me. I called. It was Mike."[18]

As with many good stories, there are slightly different versions of these events. Sill's recollection of the encounter at Norty's agrees with Leiber's in most respects, except that it has a slightly altered chronology. In Sill's version, Leiber and Stoller had already met by the time he encountered Jerry at the record store. He also said that the first thing he noticed about Leiber was his interesting genetic quirk. "When I was selling records for Modern, one of the stops I made was at Fairfax Avenue at Norty's record shop," Sill said in an interview. "I walked in there one day and this kid walks up to me, he was a clerk. I was immediately mesmerized. He had a blue eye and a brown eye." Leiber complimented Sill on his suit and on the records that he promoted, and then asked if he could show the salesman some lyrics. Sill was agreeable. "We set up a meeting and he came to my house with Mike," Sill recalled. "Mike was his partner then." Despite any discrepancies in their time lines, the important part of both recollections is not disputed. Regardless of when exactly it happened, at some point in 1950 drummer Jerry Horowitz recommended Stoller as his replacement, and a short time later Leiber contacted Stoller. Both were seventeen at the time. Leiber was finishing his last year of high school while Stoller had already enrolled in Los Angeles City College.[19]

Leiber and Stoller's first telephone conversation gave no indication that it was the beginning of a great musical association. After identifying himself, and dropping Horowitz's name, Leiber asked Stoller if he could read and write music, and then asked him if he wanted to write songs. Stoller initially resisted the idea of forming a songwriting partnership because he thought Leiber wanted to write benign, popular tunes in the vein of "How Much Is that Doggie in the Window." The pianist had no interest in cheap, commercial fare, viewing himself as a blues and jazz purist. "Jerry told me, on the phone [that] he was a songwriter and wanted to collaborate with me writing songs," Stoller said. "And that was the last thing I thought I would want to do, . . . I was sure that he meant some kinds of songs that I would hate." Despite the pushback, Leiber persisted. "[Stoller] was adamant," Leiber remembered. "He didn't want to write songs. He made it clear that he was doing me a favor by talking to me."[20]

Despite Stoller's lack of enthusiasm, he agreed to meet with Leiber, just as a courtesy. Leiber arrived at Stoller's house with a notebook full of lyrics, and it soon became apparent that the pianist had misjudged him. Like Sill, Stoller was struck by Leiber's eyes before they ever got down to business. "I opened the door and there was this smiling guy with one bright, shining blue eye, and one shining brown eye," he later said. "When I looked in his notebook and saw a line, and then ditto marks and a rhyming line, I realized they were 12 bar blues and I said, hey, I like the blues. Let's do it." Thus began one of America's premier songwriting partnerships. Leiber would concentrate on the words, and Stoller the music, and although they were white, they would bring to their work a keen, mutual appreciation of African American musical styles. "We loved the blues," Stoller said, "and what we started out to do was emulate the things that we loved the most, and the people that we loved the most." Likewise, Leiber pointed out, "Mike was essentially jazz-blues oriented, and I was more country, delta blues oriented, but we found a meeting ground, which was the blues, eight-bar, twelve bar blues phrase, which is where we came together and began writing these simple blues songs."[21]

It was an extraordinary collaborative effort. Leiber and Stoller were only teenagers, but they had a highly focused determination to compose "Black" music, even though they were white. Through the years, scores of reporters would ask them about their early working relationship and the mechanics that went into composing their music. Stoller gave one of the earliest public descriptions of their process in a 1957 newspaper article, published after they had put together their first string of hits. "We worked well together," he said. "We'd sit around, me at the piano knocking out some riffs and Jerry pacing up and down tossing out phrases. We'd improvise the song as we went along." In a later interview, Leiber confirmed Stoller's assertion with a smile. "Mike would sit down at the piano and jam, and I would just sort of walk around the room and start yelling something." The partnership also thrived despite—or perhaps because of—the opposing personalities of the partners. Leiber was outwardly more energetic and outspoken, while Stoller was more contemplative and reserved. "From the get-go our energies were different,"

Leiber said. "Mike was cautious and I was impetuous. You might even say I was reckless." Lester Sill, who witnessed the dynamic frequently, later said, "They were night and day. Mike was just a little short of comatose. Jerry was always the driver. He always had to push it."[22]

Leiber ended up enrolling in Los Angeles City College when he finished high school, but he and Stoller never had much interest in pursuing their formal education. They were too busy learning a craft that would make them famous. As a songwriting team they were prolific, working ten-hour days on a routine basis, determined to create a catalogue of blues numbers that others might want to record—and by others, they meant African American artists. Leiber later told *Rolling Stone* magazine, "What we wanted to do was try to be as good as we could at writing blues, for blues singers. Which meant exclusively Black performers, writing in the Black vernacular." Of course, they were also having fun. "Honestly, when Jerry and I first started to write, we were writing just to amuse ourselves," Stoller said. "It was done out of the love of doing it."[23]

Leiber took Stoller to meet Lester Sill, and they showed him some of their freshly minted tunes, including, a swinging, irreverent number with Old Testament references called "That's What the Good Book Says." Sill liked what he heard and set up an appointment for the boys with Modern Records. Again, there are slightly different versions of what happened next. According to Leiber and Stoller, the Bihari brothers failed to keep the appointment, so the songwriters left the building angry and went down the street to Aladdin Records, another small label specializing in African American music. There they got a commitment from Aladdin to record at least a couple of their songs. Supposedly, when Sill found out what happened, he mended fences with Modern, who also agreed to record Leiber and Stoller's work. In a later interview, Sill seemed to indicate that the initial meeting with Modern was successful, not mentioning any friction that may have developed. What lends some credit to Sill's version of the tale is that Modern released the songwriter's first two records, while Aladdin released their first chart hit.[24]

Leiber and Stoller took "That's What the Good Book Says" to Modern, and the label thought it might be a good fit for a group they knew called the Robins. The quartet was based in Los Angeles and initially included Ty Terrell, brothers Billy and Roy Richards, and Bobby Nunn. They later added tenor Carl Gardner, among others, and some of the members went on to form the Coasters. Originally called the Bluebirds, the group performed for the first time as the Robins in 1949 and was one of the first "doo-wop" groups to record. They came in and heard the song, with Leiber singing and Stoller accompanying him on the piano. They loved the tune and recorded it not long afterward. It never gained much traction and ultimately came out as a B-side, supporting another song titled "Rockin'." Rather than being discouraged by the poor showing in sales—or the fact that their writing credits on the label were misspelled as "Lieber and Stroller"—the songwriters were ecstatic. Someone had recorded one of their songs.[25]

Sill also introduced Leiber and Stoller to Gene Norman, a former disc jockey who was one of the best-known blues and jazz promoters on the West Coast. Through Norman, they met Jimmy Witherspoon, a "blues shouter" who had always been one of their favorite singers. Witherspoon was born in Arkansas in 1920, and after military service during World War II he moved to the West Coast and made his first recordings backed by Jay McShann's band. In 1947, he had a hit with "Ain't Nobody's Business," an old blues number with roots going back to the 1920s. It became his signature song. Excited to meet the singer, Leiber and Stoller gave him one of their songs, a slow blues number titled "Real Ugly Woman." Witherspoon liked it and agreed to perform it at an upcoming concert that Norman was promoting at the Shrine Auditorium in Los Angeles. Good to his word, Witherspoon sang the song, and in a stroke of luck for the songwriters, the show was being recorded. Modern put "Real Ugly Woman" out as a live single only a few weeks after they released "That's What the Good Book Says." It was not a big seller, but for the songwriters the experience was great. "I'd say Spoon is probably the best artist we've ever worked with to this day," Leiber said in a 1975 interview. "Not only is he a real professional and easy to work with, but he is a tremendous talent, too." The release of a second song gave Leiber and Stoller the confidence to shop their work around. This led them to Aladdin Records, where they were already friendly with Maxwell Davis, a studio musician and top-notch arranger who would be an important early presence in their story.[26]

Eddie and Leo Messner founded Aladdin in 1945, and like Modern, it specialized in jazz, blues, and rhythm and blues. Among the array of talent who worked with the label were Lester Young, Charles Brown, Lightnin' Hopkins, Al Hibbler, and Billie Holiday. Born in Kansas in 1916, Maxwell Davis moved to the West Coast in the early 1930s, where he played saxophone in the Fletcher Henderson Orchestra. Within a few years he established himself as one of the best sidemen in Los Angeles, as well as a talented writer and arranger, and through the years he worked with everyone. Blues icon B. B. King, who knew Davis well, later praised him as one of the unsung heroes in the world of rhythm and blues. "He was good at writing [arrangements], so good," King said. "I don't think I've ever met anyone who could write a blues [song] like Maxwell Davis. Before or since. He was unknown outside the industry, but he made a lot of records for a lot of people." The Bihari brothers later hired him away from Aladdin, and he became Modern's top producer. He worked for other labels as well. When asked about Davis in an interview years later, Stoller said, "Maxwell Davis is an unsung hero of early rhythm and blues. He produced, in effect, all of the record sessions for Aladdin records, Modern records, all the local independent rhythm and blues companies in the 1950s, late 1940s in Los Angeles."[27]

Davis liked Leiber and Stoller, and was open to listening to their songs. In turn, they admired Davis, who had recently produced the hit "Bad, Bad Whiskey" for Amos Milburn. The songwriters played him "Hard Times," a slow blues number that Davis thought might be a fit for singer Charles Brown. Brown, whose laid-back style and piano work drew comparisons to Nat King Cole, was an established performer who had recorded more than a dozen sides for Aladdin. His songs sold well, and he had recently had a big hit with a song titled "Black Night," which stayed #1 on the *Billboard* R&B charts for fourteen weeks. Leiber and Stoller visited Brown at his home and repeated the sales pitch that they had made to Davis a few days earlier. Leiber sang "Hard Times" for the singer, accompanied on the piano by Stoller. Brown liked the song and recorded it not long afterward, with Davis contributing on sax. It sold more than 80,000 copies and made the R&B top ten. For Brown it was another hit with Aladdin, but for Leiber and Stoller it was validation.[28]

With a hit song under their belt, and Lester Sill singing their praises, Leiber and Stoller began to circulate in, and were accepted by, the local blues and R&B community in Los Angeles. As had been the case on the East Coast, they felt comfortable in the Black community, and the Black community felt comfortable with them in a way that likely seemed a bit strange to the outside world. "They were amused by us, two white kids doing the blues," Leiber later told *Rolling Stone* magazine. "They thought it was goofy, a lot of fun." The young songwriters got to know many of their radio heroes, both the ones who lived in the Los Angeles area and the ones who routinely passed through on tour. "I felt black. I was black as far as I was concerned," Leiber said. "We lived a black lifestyle as young guys. We had black girlfriends for years. In a general sense, it was extreme. But not in the environment we moved in."[29]

For a couple of young men who wanted to enjoy the Black community in Los Angeles, and be players in the music industry, Leiber and Stoller's timing could not have been better. They were coming of age in a city that had recently experienced a great deal of growth and cultural upheaval, particularly in the African American community. Since before the end of the Second World War, African American immigrants had been moving into the city in waves, settling in and around Central Avenue, with the corner of Central and 41st Street being the epicenter of the district. During the day, the area was a commercial center where the city's Black community shopped. At night, it became a vibrant entertainment mecca where bars and nightclubs featured some of the best live music in the country. Just as 52nd Street in New York had been a catalyst for the advance of jazz and blues back east, Central Avenue helped foster a similar phenomenon on the West Coast. Nightspots like Club Alabam, the Dunbar Hotel, the Downbeat, and the Five-Four Ballroom hosted top talent on a consistent basis.[30]

The songwriters' timing was exceptional in another respect. The Black music that they adored was on the cusp of entering the mainstream. For decades, recordings by African American artists were classified as "race records" within the industry. They were marketed to Black audiences, although some adventurous whites also purchased them. That was one reason that Leiber and Stoller were such oddities. They were white men attempting to write modern commercial music that was defined as Black. White songwriters had tried it before, most notably during the minstrel era, composing tunes that degraded or lampooned African American life. But what Leiber and Stoller were up to was different in context. By the 1950s, great change was underway. By that time, radio stations that played African American music were more common, meaning that whites—and especially white teenagers—had access to Black music in their homes and automobiles. White teens might have had to wait until their parents were away or asleep to tune in those stations, but they could nonetheless tune in. The music industry terminology for referencing songs by African American artists was also changing. Deemed antiquated and offensive in postwar America, the terms "race records" and "race music" gave way to something more descriptive and sophisticated. In 1948, *Billboard* magazine changed its chart classification for Black recordings to "rhythm and blues," and the name caught on.

On a deeper level, the civil rights movement was beginning in earnest, ushering in a period of heightened racial awareness regarding what was right and wrong. While Black radio stations helped desegregate the airwaves, the civil rights movement would begin desegregating physical space, bringing many Blacks and whites closer together in public places, including entertainment venues. These and many other factors led to a great seismic shift in American music culture as white teenagers embraced what to them was an exciting, new style of music that was not really new at all. It was music based in the blues, with a little country, jazz, and even Tin Pan Alley thrown in. They called it rock 'n' roll, and once it hit, nothing was ever the same. It undermined existing social mores and sensitized many whites to the existence of another culture that could be celebrated rather than feared. Less than five years after Charles Brown recorded "Hard Times," Little Richard had his first hit with "Tutti Frutti," Chuck Berry began his career with "Maybelline," Elvis Presley recorded "Heartbreak Hotel," and the U.S. Supreme Court issued its decision in the landmark case *Brown v. Board of Education of Topeka.*

It was an explosive era indeed, and Leiber and Stoller took it all in. Sill continued introducing the pair to all the right people, including an energetic and well-connected producer named Ralph Bass. Born Ralph Brasso in 1911 in the Bronx to an Italian father and Jewish mother, Bass got his start with Black and White Records during the 1940s. He scouted talent and produced blues and jazz records by prominent Black artists, including Lena Horne, Roosevelt Sykes, and T-Bone Walker. He once told an interviewer, "I was a talent scout, I was a promotion man, I saw the DJs, I went to the branch offices, as well as producing records. You did everything." He traveled ceaselessly through the South, usually tagging along with blues bands, scouring the countryside for musicians and singers who had the chops to make records. He was also a visionary who understood that there might be a significant, untapped white audience for jazz and blues music. He acted on that premise and ended up being one of the pioneers who helped introduce whites to blues recordings. By the early 1950s, he was working for Federal Records, a subsidiary of King Records. Syd Nathan owned King, which had its headquarters in Cincinnati. Nathan was a smart operator who knew the business side of the record industry backward and forward, although many said he had no ear for music. He left it up to men like Bass to recruit commercially viable performers. While King launched the careers of a number of R&B acts, it also had many successful country releases.

Bass was quite a character. Although he was white, in attitude and demeanor he could be racially ambiguous, straddling the color line with relative ease. John Hartley Fox, who wrote a definitive history of King Records, described Bass as "a jive-talking wheeler-dealer, half artist and half con artist. . . . He moved freely between two parallel worlds at a time in America when relatively few people crossed the racial divide. . . . he was proudest of the role he played in bringing blacks and whites closer together through a common love for music."[31]

Bass eventually left Black and White for Savoy Records, where he supervised an early string of successful recordings for bandleader Johnny Otis and several sides from the Robins, who had recorded Leiber and Stoller's "That's What the Good Book Says" on Modern. From there, he started a seven-year association with King in the early 1950s, with Nathan giving him an ownership stake in the Federal label. At Federal, he produced the Dominoes, Esther Mae "Little Esther" Phillips, Hank Ballard and the Midnighters, and Little Willie Littlefield. Probably Bass's most famous musical coup was the signing of James Brown to Federal in 1956, beating out Chess Records, the famous Chicago blues label. Leiber and Stoller were impressed with Bass, who from their perspective had been everywhere and done everything. "[Bass] introduced us to the world of Little Esther, Little Willie Littlefield, and the great Johnny Otis," Stoller later said. "He also put on shows featuring the artists he had discovered and groomed." The two songwriters hung out with Bass's artists and started pitching tunes. Little Esther ended up recording several of their efforts, but a song that they wrote for Little Willie

Littlefield would have a lasting impact on their careers, and on American popular music.[32]

Littlefield grew up in Houston and was a born musician. As a teenager he played boogie-woogie piano to great acclaim in local nightclubs. He came to Los Angeles, and by the time he joined the Federal lineup in 1952 he had recorded more than a dozen singles, including "It's Midnight" and "Farewell," both of which made the top ten in the *Billboard* national R&B charts. Always looking for new material, Ralph Bass asked Leiber and Stoller to write a special song specifically for Littlefield. At the time, no one knew that the simple request would produce an R&B and rock 'n' roll standard that innumerable artists would later cover. According to Stoller, "One day Bass asked us to write a song about Kansas City for Little Willie Littlefield. Kansas City was the home of swing, jazz and blues—music that Jerry and I loved. It was also known as a pretty wild place."[33] The songwriters got together at Stoller's place, and Leiber came up with the song's first line: "I'm going to Kansas City, Kansas City here I come."

A bit of a free-for-all followed as the partners struggled to marry the lyrics to the music. Spirited conflict was often part of their creative process, with the tense back and forth seeming to energize them. As they composed "Kansas City," a "big fight" broke out. Leiber wanted the song to sound like a traditional blues number, something in the vein of Howlin' Wolf, while Stoller envisioned something a little brighter and more up-tempo. Leiber eventually gave in, and Stoller's melody anchored the piece. "I hated admitting I was wrong about 'Kansas City,'" Leiber said, "but that time Mike was right on the money." Once they finished, they taught "Kansas City" to Littlefield so that he could record it. The session went well, but before releasing the song Ralph Bass changed the title to "KC Loving," something that he thought was sexier and more sophisticated.[34]

Ironically, the original version of one of rock 'n' roll's most recorded songs was not a commercial success. It sold sporadically, circulating well in a few markets, but it never conquered the national charts. Regardless, it was popular with live audiences in nightclubs, which led other artists to perform and eventually record the song. Seven years after the Littlefield release, Wilbert Harrison released a version using the original Leiber and Stoller title, "Kansas City." With slightly altered lyrics, it became a #1 hit, established the song nationally, and spurred a stampede of artists who were looking to cash in. In 1959 alone, at least eight cover versions of "Kansas City" hit the airwaves by performers white and Black. In addition to Harrison's effort, Hank Ballard and the Midnighters, Rocky Olson, Little Richard, Jack Parnell, Rockin' Robin and the Rebels, Rikki Henderson, and Digby Richards all put out covers of the song that *Billboard* described as "a finger-snappin' blues with a highly contagious sound."[35] From there, the list of artists covering the tune is vast, crossing not only the color line, but including just about every musical genre. Bill Haley and His Comets, Fabian, Sammy Davis Jr., Ann-Margaret, Clyde McPhatter, and Dion all covered the song, with the Beatles accelerating the proliferation of "Kansas City" worldwide when they released their version in late 1964. Fabled bluesmen Muddy Waters, Albert King, and Little Milton all recorded "Kansas City," as did country greats George Jones and Johnny Paycheck. By 2023, at least three hundred versions of the song by different artists are believed to exist on record. More than just a successful, well-covered tune, "Kansas City" was Leiber and Stoller's first rock 'n' roll anthem.

There were more anthems to come. As time wore on, Leiber and Stoller were in growing demand. They circulated freely through the rhythm and blues community in Southern California, and their names began popping up in meeting rooms and studios where producers and performers were always on the lookout for new songs. They also started doing more than just supplying material, inching their way into studio supervision when artists cut their songs. According to Stoller, "We found that if we wrote a piece that was played as a Texas Shuffle, for example, it would more than likely end up sounding like some Mickey Mouse swing record if we weren't there to supervise. And so we became producers in self-defense." This experience on the production end of the recording process paid dividends, as artists soon sought them out not just for songs, but for musical advice as well. All this attention created the perfect storm for the creation of another rock 'n' roll epic, penned by Leiber and Stoller, interpreted by an intimidating three-hundred-pound African American woman, and finally launched into the stratosphere by another white kid who dreamed of being Black.[36]

Chapter 2 BIG MAMA

I try to sing it my own way.
Its always best to have something of your own.
I don't sing like nobody but myself.

—WILLIE MAE "BIG MAMA" THORNTON,
quoted in Michael Spörke, *Big Mama Thornton: The Life and Music*

Among the R&B movers and shakers who took notice of Leiber and Stoller was a multi-talented producer and bandleader named Johnny Otis. Otis was another white man who seemed to effortlessly immerse himself in Black culture. Always in search of new material, he had recorded one of their songs and produced several for other artists, and he would be instrumental in helping the songwriters with their next major hit. By the time they all crossed paths, he had been a fixture on the Southern California music scene for years. He knew everyone in Los Angeles, and would be another key player in the "Hound Dog" story.

Johnny Otis was born Ioannis Alexandres Veliotes to Greek immigrants in Vallejo, California, on December 29, 1921. He grew up in Berkeley, where his parents owned a grocery store. According to government records, his father, Alexander, came to the United States in 1903 at age fifteen and later served with an artillery unit during the First World War. His mother, Irene Kiskakes, entered the country with relatives in 1911, when she was ten years old. The two married in 1920 and had three children. Johnny was the oldest, followed by sister Dorothy and baby brother Nicholas. The family lived on Dohr Street in Berkeley, quartered on the upper floor of the modest building that housed the grocery store. All the Veliotes were musical. Alexander sang and his wife played the mandolin, Johnny taught himself drums, Nicholas was proficient on the clarinet, and Dorothy played the cello.

By the time Johnny was in his teens, his neighborhood was predominantly African American. Black culture was all around him during his formative years, and he soaked it in to the point that for the rest of his life he claimed to live as if he had been born as an African American. "My dad was a grocer in the black community in Berkeley," he later said. "He was a big-hearted guy who didn't understand about racism. Everybody I came into contact with as a kid, all my playmates, were black. I didn't know we were white or black." When he was around thirteen, a school counselor told him that it was time that he began hanging around with whites instead of Blacks, and Otis responded by ending his formal education. "After that I left and never came back to school," he said. "I never felt white. I wouldn't leave black culture to go to heaven. It's richer, more rewarding and fulfilling for me." He later married an African American woman, attended Black churches, became involved in civil rights issues, and rarely bothered to correct those who assumed that he was a light-skinned African American man. When asked directly about his race, he liked to say that he was "Black by persuasion," and later told an interviewer, "I don't think its so unique in America for white kids to grow up with black youngsters and come up together as brothers and sisters, what might be unique is to not veer away. I could not veer away." In the introduction to Otis's 1968 book, *Listen to the Lambs,* African American saxophonist and bandleader Preston Love gave his take on the unusual situation, stating, "Even after more than twenty-seven years of the closest personal ties, I am intrigued by the fact that my friend is genetically white, but in all other respects completely black."[1]

When interviewers later asked Otis about his musical influences growing up, he always credited the blues that he heard on his block as a kid, and singled out an African American neighbor living across the street who was a railroad porter. Because of his job, the man traveled around the country, and always seemed to return to the neighborhood with a couple of blues records under his arm. He hosted raucous parties at his home, during which music and laughter spilled out into the street. "He would bring back those old seventy-eights," Otis recalled. "I tell you what I heard as a kid that influenced me. I didn't know who the artist was at the time, but it turned out to be 'Terraplane Blues' by Robert Johnson." Another turning point in Otis's life came in 1939, when he saw Count Basie's orchestra perform at the Golden Gate Exposition in San Francisco. Hailed by the press as "The sepia King of Harlem," Basie and his band were at the top of their game, and for Otis their performance represented a musical epiphany. After watching the group, and particularly drummer Jo Jones, Otis fixed a career path in music. "After I saw him," he said, "I wanted to be a drummer."[2]

Otis's first foray into the professional music world was with another young Bay Area musician named Otis Matthews. Matthews was nineteen months older, and his parents had moved to Oakland from Texas not long before he was born in 1920. Later on, some Johnny Otis biographies would state that the Matthews family hailed from the Mississippi Delta, although census records do not seem to support the claim. Other records indicate that they may have originally been Louisiana natives. Regardless, the family lived on 7th Street in Oakland, and Otis visited them regularly once he and Matthews met and became friends. Matthews asked Otis to play drums in his band, Count Otis Matthews and his West Oakland Houserockers. It was a loose, six-piece ensemble that featured Matthews on piano, with the nickname "Count" as an homage to Count Basie. Johnny Otis later described the group as a "barrelhouse, boogie-woogie little band" that played mainly blues at house parties for tips, food, and the occasional jug of wine.[3] His time with the Houserockers did not last long, but it gave him a musical foundation on which to build.

In 1941, Otis married Phyllis Walker after eloping to Reno, Nevada, where interracial marriage was allowed. Looking for work, he ended up in Denver, Colorado, where he officially adopted the professional name Johnny Otis. The new name sounded more polished, and "Otis" was easier to pronounce than Veliotis. He later credited childhood playmates with the original idea for his stage moniker. "The kids at school kind of made that decision for me," he said. "They decided not to deal with trying to remember how to pronounce [Johnny Veliotes]. They would say, 'Johnny Otis,' and that's the way it stuck." While in Denver, Otis signed on as drummer with an African American band led by George Morrison. Morrison had toured for years before settling in the city, where he and different configurations of his group stayed busy playing the local country club, amusement parks, and private parties. While performing with Morrison's band, Otis met Preston Love, who played saxophone with Lloyd Hunter's Serenaders, a popular "territory band" that had stopped in Denver for a month-long engagement. *Territory band* was a term used to describe the touring dance bands of the era that crisscrossed many of the Great Plains and western states. Otis and Love hit it off immediately, bonding over their mutual love of Count Basie. "Naturally, it didn't take long for Johnny Otis and me to gravitate toward each other," Love later recalled. "Johnny had a greater gift of expression than me, which was even more fascinating to me, but he deferred to me because of his preoccupation with the mystique of African Americans. . . . Johnny's entire musical interest was black music." Not long afterward, Lloyd Hunter's regular drummer was drafted into the military, and Love arranged for Otis to audition for the vacant spot. Hunter was impressed, and suddenly Otis had a new gig.[4]

For Otis, joining the Serenaders was a step up from a good band that was satisfied playing in the Denver area to a more dynamic touring group that already had a significant regional following. It also represented further immersion in the African American culture that he adored. The world in which he lived was virtually all Black, and he seemed completely comfortable there. He traveled day and night with African Americans, stayed with his bandmates in segregated hotels, socialized with African Americans wherever he went, and, after tours ended, came home to an African American wife. "I gained firsthand experience on what it was like in the Black-territory band culture," he later said. "The older men and women in the territory bands acted as role models and teachers to the young musicians starting their climb." For Otis, it was a smooth assimilation given the era. Most people who saw the Serenaders perform simply assumed that Otis was a light-skinned Black man, because to assume otherwise seemed crazy. "I was never viewed as a white kid," Otis later said. "It was unheard of. There wouldn't be such a thing, a white kid playing in black bands."[5]

Opportunity knocked for Otis in 1943 in the form of an invitation to join Harlan Leonard's Kansas City Rockets. A veteran of the road since he was a teenager, Leonard hailed from Kansas City and had played alongside Count Basie in the Bennie Moten Band during the 1930s. When that band broke up, both men formed their own outfits, and while Basie became better known nationally, Leonard's band drew good crowds wherever they toured. They were headquartered in Los Angeles for an extended engagement at Club Alabam on Central Avenue in 1943 when their regular drummer left the group. As the story goes, it was Nat King Cole and singer Jimmy Witherspoon who recommended that Leonard take on Otis, who they had crossed paths with many times on the road. Spurred on by several other friends, Otis took a train to California and signed on with the Rockets. For the young drummer, Central Avenue in Los Angeles represented the big time. "I was thrilled to become the drummer in Harlan Leonard's band in Los Angeles at Club Alabam," he later said. "I got there in '43 and at that time the Avenue was swinging. It was like a transplanted Harlem Renaissance."[6]

Club Alabam was the hottest joint on Central Avenue, and it offered Otis a great deal of exposure. He mixed easily with other musicians in the city and made contacts that benefited him for the rest of his life. Leonard's contract with the club eventually ended, and when his band moved on, Otis stayed in Los Angeles, where there was no shortage of drumming work. In 1945 he got another break when Curtis Mosby, who owned Club Alabam, insisted that he recruit his own band. According to Otis, this new opportunity presented itself by accident one night when he went to the club to see another act and ran into Mosby, who had already had a few drinks. The place was crowded and the club owner was sitting at a table with several community movers and shakers. He called Otis over and loudly told his guests that Otis was going to recruit and lead a new group that would serve as the house band at the club. Mosby was not really serious, but the *Los Angeles Sentinel,* a Black newspaper, reported the development for all to read. Rather than lose face or look silly, Mosby decided to make good on his proclamation. "Look, now we gotta put a band together," he reportedly told Otis.[7]

Otis recruited a top-notch group to play at the club and elsewhere. "I was able to get some great players," he said. "It was a big bop swing band patterned after [Count] Basie." The club hosted big crowds that included everyone who was anyone in West Coast rhythm and blues. Nationally known touring musicians like Charlie Parker and Miles Davis sat in with the band when they passed through town, and record company executives and talent scouts were frequent guests. Otis Rene, who owned Excelsior Records, a small jazz label, came into the club one night and was impressed enough with Otis's band to bring them into the studio. They cut "Harlem Nocturne," by Earle Hagan, in the fall of 1945. It turned out to be a hit, and Otis took the band out on the road. "We played all over the country," he recalled. "We played with the Ink Spots on their national tour, with Louis Jordan, and Nat Cole. We played a lot of theaters, went everywhere for about a year."[8]

When he returned to Los Angeles, Otis with three partners opened the Barrelhouse, a popular nightclub near the corner of 107th Street and Wilmington in Watts. He paired back his band and began playing more blues than jazz, drawing large crowds just like he had at Club Alabam. Otis signed with Savoy Records in 1949, and the next year he cut a string of hits including "Double-Crossing Blues," "Mistrustin' Blues," "Rockin' Blues," "Cry Baby," and "Cupid's Boogie," which led to him receiving *Billboard* magazine's "Cash Box Award" for "making the most money for juke box operators" around the country. Two years later, he moved to Mercury Records, where his success continued, particularly as a producer and arranger. At the Barrelhouse and on the road, he auditioned young musicians and singers, functioning as a talent scout for multiple labels. In Los Angeles, he promoted talent shows that gave some performers their first opportunity to sing in front of a crowd. "The Barrelhouse was something," Otis said. "It was an impressive place and we had the talent shows and a lot of good talent was happening there." Among those he discovered during the 1950s were Little Esther Phillips, Hank Ballard, Jackie Wilson, Johnny Ace, Little Willie John, and the Robins, who recorded one of Leiber and Stoller's early tunes.

Otis also put together one of the first successful R&B package tours, known at various times as the Savoy Barrelhouse Caravan, the California Rhythm and Blues Caravan, or simply the Johnny Otis Show. Of all the performers who were part of that effort, Little Esther's star shone the brightest. "As for Little Esther," a reviewer from the *Pittsburgh (Pa.) Courier* wrote at the time, "she really has a voice. It rivals Dinah Washington's for bell-like clearness and distinctive qualities. She can really sing the blues, and with feeling." The show was very successful, a hot ticket regardless of what city the troupe visited. While they played primarily to Black audiences, the show also attracted whites to some venues. The caravan enhanced Otis's reputation not only as a bandleader, but as an important figure in the world of African American entertainment. "I think Johnny's biggest thing was being able to handle people," Ralph Bass later said. "He has a kind of charisma about him that attracts people to him, and they believe him. . . . A natural leader-type thing." In every city there were promoters, managers, and hustlers—some legitimate, some unsavory, and some a combination of both—who wanted Otis to give one of their local artists a spot on his program. Among the most infamous was a rough and tumble impresario from Houston named Don Robey.[9]

Born in Houston on November 1, 1903, to an African American father and a white mother, Don Deadric Robey was a formidable character. He grew up on the streets of Houston's Fifth Ward, and his rise to prominence was shadowy to say the least. An aggressive hustler from the outset, he quit school in the eleventh grade to pursue a career as a professional gambler, and he also worked a day job as a salesman for a liquor distributor. According to some, these associations led him into the world of organized crime, and in the future his aggressive tactics as a promoter and record executive lent credence to the notion that he was well connected to the "Black mafia" in Texas and elsewhere. During the 1930s he ran nightclubs in Houston, including the Sweet Dreams Café, the Lenox Club, and the Harlem Grille, and established a successful taxi business. Rumor had it that he was a major partner in gambling operations in the Black community, and his knack for always having large, mysterious sums of investment capital on hand seemed to bear this out. In the nightclubs, he booked top-flight African American talent, which led him into the promotion business. Soon he was booking bands all over Texas and along the "Chitlin' Circuit," a network of African American performance venues that sprang up in the South and elsewhere during the first half of the twentieth century. According to Preston Lauterbach, author of *The Chitlin' Circuit: And the Road to Rock 'n' Roll,* "Robey routinely booked the country's top black jazz orchestras, including Duke Ellington and Ella Fitzgerald. Robey put Houston on the map. . . . He carried the city from the edge of the hinterlands in the black entertainment world to its status as a regular stop for premier 'colored' stars."[10]

In February 1946, Robey opened an upscale nightspot, the Bronze Peacock, on the corner of Erastus and Wylie Streets in Houston. He hired first-class chefs to prepare meals served to patrons at tables covered with spotless white tablecloths. From all accounts, the club featured the best of everything, including stage shows with famous entertainers and side rooms where patrons could gamble illegally. The place was also unusual because it attracted an integrated audience, including well-to-do whites with political connections who enjoyed the entertainment and intrigues that the club offered without much risk of repercussions. Evelyn Johnson, Robey's business partner and confidant, ran the day-to-day operations. "We had an emcee, comedians, bands, featured singers, the whole nine yards," she later recalled. "White people, important people, came in there. Segregation laws were not enforced with those people." Well-known acts like T-Bone Walker, Louis Jordan, and Ruth Brown performed in the club's large showroom, as did young, unknown musicians and singers whose talents Robey hoped to capitalize on.[11]

One night in 1947, Clarence "Gatemouth" Brown filled in for an ill T-Bone Walker at the Bronze Peacock. He impressed Robey to such an extent that Robey decided to take him on as a client and manage his career. Brown signed with Aladdin Records, but Robey grew dissatisfied with the label's treatment of his discovery. He decided to record Brown himself, and in 1949 he established Peacock Records in Houston. Initially, he recorded at the Audio Company of America (ACA) studio in the city, but in the early 1950s, after acquiring Memphis-based Duke Records, he closed the Bronze Peacock and converted the space into a studio, as well as the headquarters of his labels, publishing company, and booking agency. According to Robey business associate John Green, "They took [the Bronze Peacock] and converted it into a recording studio and the booking office was there, too. And they had a pressing plant in back, and pressed the records right there. . . . And that building was the base for all of Peacock [and Duke]." With regard to the actual recording space, guitarist Milton Hopkins later recalled, "The studio at Peacock was medium sized, not a huge studio . . . but if need be, you could assemble a twelve to fourteen-piece orchestra in there. It would have been kind of tight, but it could happen." Robey's empire grew, with his holdings eventually including the Songbird, Back Beat, and Sure Shot labels. He became an important figure in the rhythm and blues and gospel world, recording Bobby Bland, Johnny Ace, and Junior Parker along with gospel stalwarts the Dixie Hummingbirds, the Mighty Clouds of Joy, the Swan Silvertones, and the Five Blind Boys from Mississippi. Although their relationship did not last long, Robey also made early recordings of "Little Richard" Penniman, one of rock 'n' roll's founding fathers, and for a time Robey's booking agency handled B. B. King.[12]

Much of Robey's success was built on a combination of street smarts and pure intimidation that sometimes turned violent. While some musicians later sang his praises for getting them started, others associated with Robey's business interests portrayed him as a much darker figure. "He was just like a character out of *Guys and Dolls,*" one associate said. "He'd have a bunch of heavy guards around him all the time, carrying pistols and that kind of stuff, like a czar of the negro underworld." Robey's own weapon of choice was a 45 caliber handgun that some claimed he unholstered and placed on his desk as he negotiated deals. He was known for issuing threats and provoking physical altercations in order to get his point across. Little Richard claimed that Robey beat him up during a dispute over royalties. "He jumped on me, knocked me down and kicked me in the stomach," the colorful singer said many years later. "Right there in the office he beat me up. Knocked me out in the first round!" Albert Collins, who never recorded with Robey but was booked for live shows through his agency, agreed that the promoter was a violent man. "He'd hit you, man, put his gun in your face," Collins said. "That's the way he did that kind of thing. He was a pretty heavy dude."[13]

Robey was also a shrewd and ruthless businessman, quick to recognize cash flow opportunities. He had a habit—some would say an obsession—with tying up the publishing rights to music and assigning himself songwriting credits (sometimes under the alias Deadric Malone) for tunes that he had nothing to do with composing. Producers and labels taking advantage of songwriters was a fairly common practice, but Robey seemed to be especially proficient at it, purchasing for a pittance the rights to music from young songwriters who did not understand the business end of the music industry. "Singers loved him. Writers were the ones who got screwed," Don Head, who recorded for Robey, later said. "He was bad about that. Most of those songs were written by other people. Don would give them 25 or 50 bucks and they'd let him have their songs." Jerry Leiber, who more than once felt the sting of Robey's business tactics, later told an interviewer, "Don't be fooled by old publicity pictures of Robey in a suit and tie with black-rimmed glasses, like a legit businessman. Just like those jive-ass evangelist preachers, he didn't pay anybody." When all was said and done, over a career that spanned thirty years, Robey held copyrights on hundreds of songs. Although his rough tactics generated critics, others credited Robey with giving African American artists a place to record, and for launching the careers of many successful Black musicians. He built an empire during a period when Jim Crow segregation worked against the average African American entrepreneur. "He might have ripped me off," Gatemouth Brown later said, "but if it wasn't for Don Robey, nobody would've ever heard of me."[14]

Robey was relentless in his search for talent, and his ambitions as a music mogul knew no bounds. At recording sessions, he sometimes brought in studio musicians who were under contract elsewhere, and then changed or omitted their names in the record credits. He visited local clubs and sent out scouts to recruit musicians and singers. Young, unknown performers were always a commodity because they tended to work cheap, and they did not ask too many questions about song copyrights and royalty payments. Local taverns and juke joints in Houston and elsewhere were filled with fledgling entertainers so desperate to make it that they were blind to business irregularities that might affect their future. Robey was well aware of their naivete, and took full advantage whenever he could. While the sheer force of his personality led to much of his success, he was also quick to listen to those whose opinions he respected when they recommended new talent. He ruled his empire with an iron fist, but was always open to the ideas of others when it came to the music itself.

Among the Houston clubs through which talent passed on a regular basis was the Eldorado Ballroom, located at the corner of Elgin and Dowling Streets in Houston's Third Ward. By the time Don Robey established the Bronze Peacock in the 1940s, the Eldorado Ballroom had been hosting upscale entertainment for years. Owners Anna and Clarence Dupree were successful businesspeople and pillars of Houston's African American community. They had established the club in 1939, christening it the "home of happy feet," a nickname that they borrowed from Harlem's famous Savoy Ballroom. Like the Peacock, the "Rado" hosted national acts and talented locals on a regular basis in its main room, which featured high ceilings, neon lights, and a spacious dance floor. "The Eldorado was definitely a venue of some style and substance," one observer later said. "It was a place where people could dress up and be treated well. . . . For the Duprees, the Eldorado was an opportunity to add to their business ventures, but it also was a way for them to do something for their community."[15] Don Robey was enjoying a night out at the club in the early 1950s when he ran across an impressive female singer who immediately commanded attention. Her name was Willie Mae Thornton.

Willie Mae "Big Mama" Thornton was born December 11, 1926, in Ariton, Alabama, a tiny hamlet of six hundred residents just south of Montgomery. Her father, George, was a Baptist minister and her mother, Mattie, kept house and raised Willie Mae and her five siblings. When she was a child, Willie Mae moved with her family to nearby Troy, Alabama, where her father continued to preach. Her mother passed away in 1939, and within a year Willie Mae was living with cousins in Starr Hill, another small community near Montgomery. In interviews as an adult, she sometimes claimed that she was born and grew up in Montgomery, probably because it was the only city of any size nearby. Like many African American performers who made a name for themselves with secular music as adults, religious music was an early influence on Thornton. "My mother, she was a Christian, hard working woman," she once told an interviewer. "She sang Christian songs. . . . I used to go to church a lot." Thornton later said that the death of her mother served as a catalyst for her decision to start singing blues music. "I really got the blues in '39 when I lost my mother," she said. "I didn't know what to do. . . . At the time I was listening to Big Maceo [Merriweather]'s 'Worried Life Blues,' and I said, 'I think I want to sing that,' and I did." She also cited Bessie Smith and Lizzie "Memphis Minnie" Douglas as early influences. In rural Alabama, there were few outlets for a fourteen-year-old girl to showcase her talents as a blues singer, but fate intervened one night at a local juke joint where Thornton worked cleaning spittoons and sweeping up. When the regular singer failed to show up, the owner allowed Thornton to sing a few numbers. It was her first brush with nightclub singing and she loved it.[16]

In 1941, Sammy Green's Hot Harlem Review, a touring variety show featuring "gags, songs and dances" stopped in Montgomery for a show at the Pekin Theater, one of the city's premier Black entertainment venues. The Atlanta-based company was a typical touring troupe of the period, featuring actors, singers, dancers, comedians, and around fifty musicians. They usually performed two shows a day, each lasting between two and three hours. At the time, the outfit needed to add a female singer, and the theater organized a series of auditions for local talent. Although still only fourteen years old, Thornton showed up and begged to be heard. The tour manager, who was skeptical at first, finally relented and let her sing. Some sources say that "Diamond Teeth" Mary Smith McClain, who performed with the troupe and was songstress Bessie Smith's half-sister, had a hand in getting the youngster the audition. Regardless, Thornton made an immediate impression. Performing in a pair of jeans with one leg rolled up, she sang a Louis Jordan song called "G.I. Jive" and Big Maceo's "Worried Life Blues." More than twenty other singers auditioned, but in the end the company hired the teenager.[17]

The Hot Harlem Review pulled out of Montgomery with Willie Mae Thornton as part of the show. They traveled the Deep South and occasionally into Texas in rolling stock that included two large buses and an equipment truck. "We went to Atlanta and Birmingham," she later recalled, "Columbus, Georgia, Macon, Georgia, South Carolina, Florida. We just toured practically everywhere. . . . I started before the war. Then, after the war broke out, we went touring through Texas." Sammy Green billed her as the "New Bessie Smith," and in addition to her singing skills, she played harmonica and learned the drums while on tour. She was a natural talent and a completely self-made performer. "I never had no one teach me nothing," she later said. "I never went to school for music or nothing. . . . I taught myself to sing and to blow harmonica and even play drums by watching other people. I can't read music, but I know where I'm singing! If I hear a blues I like, I try to sing it my own way."[18]

Thornton remained with the Hot Harlem Review for several years, playing theaters and juke joints as she honed her skills as a performer. In addition to her booming voice, she was an intimidating physical presence both on and off stage. Thornton was six feet tall and seemed to gain more weight with each tour, which is how she earned her professional name "Big Mama." She loved to drink and curse, and had a habit of wearing mostly men's clothing, which generated rumors about her sexuality. While she sometimes wore dresses onstage and for promotional photographs, she seemed most comfortable in overalls or blue jeans, with shirts and hats styled for men. Bluesman David "Honeyboy" Edwards first encountered Thornton in Houston, later remarking, "She was big then, too, good-sized. The first time I saw her she was just walking down the street in the Fourth Ward, wearing big blue jeans and a man's hat cocked on the side of her head. . . . Before she got started, she played on the streets and in the juke joints just like a man." Bandleader Johnny Otis, who later helped guide her career, liked to tell the story that although he could sometimes talk her into wearing dresses onstage, she often wore blue jeans and cowboy boots underneath. Regardless of the clothes she wore, Thornton had a confident stage presence, often exchanging banter with audiences before overwhelming them with her musical delivery. "I like my old downhome singing with the feeling," she said. "My singing comes from experience, my own experience, my own feeling. I got my own feelings for everything."[19]

In 1948 fate intervened for Thornton in the form of a dispute over money with the Hot Harlem Review's management. The falling out took place during a tour stop in Houston, and the singer decided to leave the group and settle in the city. She found work here and there, singing with various bands, and also held odd jobs to make ends meet. In 1950 she made her first recording, a raucous but forgotten blues number titled "All Right Baby." The record was credited as the Harlem Stars and released on a tiny local label called E&W. About the same time, Thornton caught the attention of saxophonist and bandleader Joe "Papoose" Fritz, who hired her to sing with his group. The band performed regularly at the Eldorado Ballroom, which is where Don Robey first saw her. Recognizing her potential, Robey signed her to an exclusive, five-year contract and she moved over to the Bronze Peacock, where she sang with the house band. According to Fritz, "She . . . joined my band as a vocalist—everybody had to have a female vocalist in those days. I paid her $50 a night until Don Robey stole her away from me."[20]

Robey began managing Thornton's career in hopes of making her one of the pillars of Peacock Records. He placed Joe Scott in charge of her first recording session, which took place at the ACA studio in Houston in early 1951. Scott was a trumpet player, bandleader, and Peacock's most talented arranger. He helped Robey with studio sessions and, in general, served as his right-hand man when it came to producing the music that ended up on record. He also served as a mentor for young artists, teaching them what the recording process was all about and helping them navigate the intricacies of studio work. "When I met him, I didn't know anything about music," one Houston guitarist who worked regularly with Scott later said. "After two weeks, I was reading chord diagrams." Scott's band backed Thornton on "I'm All Fed Up" and "Partnership Blues," the two sides of her first release. The exact origins of the songs are unclear, but Robey took the writing credit on both.[21]

Initially, Thornton's recording career at Peacock sputtered. "I'm All Fed Up" and "Partnership Blues" failed to sell in large numbers, even after Robey placed an ad in the February 3, 1951, edition of *Billboard* trumpeting their release. Thornton's sometimes crude ways also did not endear her to Evelyn Johnson, who, from the standpoint of daily operations, ran Robey's music empire. She tried to buy Thornton new clothes to wear when she performed, in hopes of crafting for her a more respectable image on stage, but Thornton would have none of it. Johnson saw Thornton as a "female thug," later stating that the singer "was very blunt, and she used a lot of bad language. She wore khaki pants, plaid shirts all the time. Part of it was her overall mental thing. Part of it was her exposure, and it was just her. She was very prone to say 'I ain't wearing that.'"[22]

In late 1951 Robey sent Thornton into the studio again, this time backed by the Bill Harvey Band. Harvey was a Mississippi native who cut his teeth as a saxophonist and bandleader on Beale Street in Memphis, becoming a local legend in that city. According to B. B. King, Harvey was "the George Washington of Memphis musicians. . . . a brilliant bandleader and arranger and tenor saxophonist." Always in need of good producers and arrangers, Robey signed Harvey and he came to Houston, where he and his band backed many Peacock recording artists. With Harvey, Thornton recorded "Let Your Tears Fall Baby" and "No Jody for Me," both of which Peacock released in December of 1951, with Robey again taking writing credits. Neither song resonated with the record-buying public, but they did get a very brief mention in the December 29, 1951, issue of *Billboard.* In assessing both records, a reviewer wrote that "Let Your Tears Fall Baby" provided "a good shouting vocal from Thornton, plus solid ork [orchestra] background," while "No Jody for Me" was judged a "better-than-average blues." Lukewarm praise that again did not live up to Robey's expectations. Thornton was popular in the Houston area and could draw crowds in local clubs, but establishing a national reputation for the singer remained an elusive goal. Her next recordings with

Harvey's band, "Every Time I Think of You" and "Mischievous Boogie," represented a step back, getting very little notice outside Houston.[23]

Not long after these disappointments, Thornton's luck began to change. The famous bandleader Johnny Otis and his touring review arrived in Houston, sending a ripple of excitement through the city's entertainment community. Otis was more than an entertainer, as everyone in the music business knew. Attention from the bandleader could boost a struggling artist's career. Wherever Otis went, local talent brokers tried to sell him on one of their singers. The idea was, if Otis liked what he heard, he might take the singer with him on tour, generating national exposure for the artist and, ultimately, income for the manager and label involved in the singer's career. While Don Robey was certainly better known and better connected than most of the record men who regularly approached Otis, he was no different from them in that he was always looking for a new way to make another buck on the artists whose careers he controlled. In Houston, Robey asked Otis to audition a handful of his acts, and Otis agreed to do so. Despite Robey's harsh reputation, the two men forged a relationship that led to Otis scouting talent for Peacock, and later recording several songs with the label. "He and I got along," Otis later said. "I don't know why, but we did. I saw him just run roughshod over people, but he didn't do that to me."[24]

Robey sent several singers in to see Otis, but the bandleader saw potential in only two. One was Marie Adams, Peacock's most successful artist to date. She had recently scored a hit with "I'm Gonna Play the Honky Tonks," which climbed to #3 on the *Billboard* R&B chart. The other was Willie Mae Thornton. Otis decided to take Thornton with him on tour, despite warnings that her appeal might be geographically limited. "I was told that she would do great in the South, but [in the North] they probably won't understand her," Otis said. "But one of the next jobs was Boston and she fractured everybody in the joint. . . . fast blues and slow blues, you know, and blues ballads." Otis's show toured the country, and a stop at the Apollo Theater in New York City in late April of 1952 marked a turning point in Thornton's career. At the time, the caravan included Otis's band, with singers Little Esther, Mel Walker, and Thornton, along with several dancers and popular comedian Dewey "Pigmeat" Markham. Little Esther was the featured attraction, drawing a good deal of attention in the entertainment press in the days leading up to the show. "Little Esther, Otis Band Headline New Apollo Bill," one newspaper headline read, with the accompanying article lauding Little Esther as "one of the country's great blues singers." A promotional photograph of Little Esther also appeared with the announcement. The same article mentioned Thornton only once in passing, describing her as "a driving blues singer who is a house-rocker." It was apparent that she enjoyed only "opening act" status with the group, but that would soon change.[25]

The engagement at the Apollo ran for several days, but Thornton stole the show on the first night with a rousing version of the Dominoes' "Have Mercy, Baby." The fallout from the appearance caused Otis to alter his onstage lineup for the rest of the tour. Instead of opening shows, Thornton would be closing them. Years later, Thornton told her version of the events to noted rock critic Ralph Gleason:

> I went with Johnny Otis and we played the Apollo Theater in New York, and that's where they made their mistake. They put me on first! I wasn't out there to put no one off stage. I was out there to get known and I did! I stopped the show. They had to put the curtain down. Little Esther never got on that first show. That's when they put my name in lights. Mr. Schiffman, the manager of the Apollo, came backstage hollerin' to Johnny Otis and poking me in the arms with his fingers. "You said you had a star and you got a star! You got to put her on to close the show."[26]

While Thornton's later recollection may have exaggerated the story a bit, there is no doubt that her first appearance at the Apollo changed the dynamics of Johnny Otis's road show. By the time the troupe made it to the West Coast for a series of shows three months later, Thornton was receiving the lion's share of the press coverage. "Still the show-stopper with the review," one Los Angeles correspondent wrote, "is Willie Mae Thornton, Johnny's robust blues shouter." It was also at the Apollo where manager Frank Schiffman reportedly gave Thornton the nickname "Big Mama," because of her booming voice and the way that her six-foot, full-figured frame contrasted physically with the much smaller Little Esther.[27]

Part of Don Robey's arrangement with Johnny Otis held that Otis would try to find something suitable for Thornton to record. Back on his home turf in Los Angeles, he decided to take her into the studio, but he needed something fresh for her to sing, which led him to approach Jerry Leiber and Mike Stoller, the young songsmiths who had written "Kansas City" for Little Willie Littlefield. Otis already knew Leiber and Stoller, having recorded one of their songs himself and produced several more for other artists. While Otis and the songwriters seemed to work well together, and in the future they would say complementary things about one another in the press, the sometimes contentious nature of writing credits and royalties put a strain on the relationship. Otis later said that while working with the songwriters he sometimes helped them compose, a claim that Leiber and Stoller disputed. "We wrote a lot of things together," Otis later said. "I met them here in Los Angeles through a record distributor. They were young kids. . . . They would bring in songs. They would write the songs and I would rewrite the songs with them." The situation eventually led to litigation.[28]

According to Otis, he had to rewrite some of Leiber and Stoller's songs because the young songwriters had an immature understanding of race relations. Otis pointed out that while the pair had obvious sympathy for African Americans, and always claimed that they "felt Black," they could never write music from a Black perspective. It was impossible. "For instance," Otis later recalled, "once they had a song that had 'razor cutting' and 'gin drinking' and 'dice shooting' [in the lyrics]. They didn't understand that this was derogatory for black people. They just didn't understand it. They were young guys who meant well. They were not racist in the true sense of the word." Others echoed the same sentiment. Otis's old friend Preston Love later told an interviewer, "[Leiber and Stoller] were little Jewish kids who brought in the typical young kid's version of black music. It was all corned up. They had dice shooting in there, watermelon-eating, 'dat boy,' and all that. It wasn't characteristic true black music, and Johnny used to have to moderate the derogatory stuff."[29]

Despite these complications, Otis apparently had confidence in Leiber and Stoller, and felt that they might be a good fit with Willie Mae Thornton. Otis invited the songwriters to his home, specifically the garage behind his house that he used as a rehearsal space, so that they could meet Thornton and hear her sing. For Leiber and Stoller, their first encounter with her was memorable to say the least. "When Jerry and I arrived and heard her start

Left to right, Johnny Otis, Willie Mae "Big Mama" Thornton, and Don Robey. Otis and Robey helped steer Thornton's early career, and Otis later made an unsuccessful legal claim that he cowrote "Hound Dog." Micheal Ochs Archives/Getty Images.

to sing, we looked at each other in amazement," Stoller said. "In her combat boots and overalls, she was formidable and a bit frightening. Her voice was a force of nature. Big Mama was absolutely magnificent." Leiber agreed, later telling an interviewer, "We saw Big Mama and she knocked me cold. She looked like the biggest, baddest, saltiest chick you would ever see. And she was mean, a 'lady bear,' as they used to call 'em. She must have been 350 pounds." Otis asked the songwriters if they had anything that Thornton might use, and they replied that they did not, but that they could come up with something in short order.[30]

Leiber and Stoller left the garage and went back to Stoller's house inspired. According to Leiber, his mission was clear in his mind. He wanted to write a song about a strong woman standing up with impunity to a shifty man. "I had to write a song for her that basically said, 'Go fuck yourself,'" he said. "But how to do it without actually saying it? And how to do it telling a story? I couldn't just have a song full of expletives." Once they started working, they put the song together quickly. Both men later claimed that it took just a few minutes. "We jumped in my car, my '37 Plymouth, and drove back to my house," Stoller said. "By the time we got there, Jerry was already cooking on a lyric. And I went in and started playing the piano and we had the song finished in about ten or twelve minutes. We drove back to Johnny's house and presented it to Big Mama." Back at Otis's place, Thornton grabbed the lyric sheet out of Leiber's hands and began reading over it. She later told an interviewer that the songwriters gave her the lyrics written "on the back of a paper bag," but this may have been a joking comment related to the speed with which they composed the number rather than a literal description of the paper on which Leiber wrote the lyrics.[31]

Commenting later on the actual process of penning the tune, Leiber said that at first he used the phrase "hound dog" only as a "dummy lyric," just words to play with until he could think of something better, but Stoller liked it, so they kept it. "You ain't nothing but a hound dog" became the first line of the song. This was all while they were still in the car, on their way home from Johnny Otis's house. Once they got to Stoller's place they took the words "hound dog" and ran with them. According to Leiber:

> We walked into Mike's house, and he walked over—and I will never forget it, the moment is indelibly etched on my memory—he walked over to the piano, and he had a cigarette in this mouth, and the smoke was curling up into his eye, and he kept it there and he was playing, and he was grooving with the rhythm, and he was grooving, grooving, grooving, and we locked into one place. Lyrical content, syllabically, locked in to the rhythm of the piano, and we knew we had it. . . . And he was singing 'You ain't nothing but a hound dog,' and I said 'yeah, yeah, yeah.' That's it.[32]

Once Thornton read the lyric sheet, she rehearsed the song with the band, but at first she did not sing it the way that the songwriters intended. This touched off a humorous but edgy confrontation with Jerry Leiber. Slightly different versions of the story have been told through the years, but in all of them Thornton initially did not appreciate Leiber's input on her performance. She apparently sang the song more as a "crooner," with Leiber suggesting that she change her delivery. "We wanted her to growl it," Stoller said, "which she rejected at first." According to Leiber, after he made the suggestion, Thornton "turned and faced me with a fury that knocked me on my heels." The gist of her response was that no skinny white kid was going to tell her how to sing the blues, and she punctuated her message with an obscene gesture that had the band doubled over laughing. Otis, the consummate producer, stepped in and had Leiber sing the song himself for a skeptical Thornton and the band. "Big Mama liked Johnny's idea," Stoller said. "She stood there with her arms folded, ready to laugh at the white teenager trying to sing the blues. As I played, Jerry sang the first few lines. . . . Suddenly the joke was over. Big Mama heard how Jerry was singing the thing. She heard the rough and tough of the song, just as important, the implicit sexual humor. In short, she got it." This version of "Hound Dog" was gritty, with lyrics that were different from those that Elvis Presley would make famous three years later. In Big Mama's version, she ordered her antagonist to "quit snoopin' 'round my door," while Presley later admonished his for "cryin' all the time." Her version was a blues classic because of the force of her delivery, while Presley's was more of a novelty number, although it was powerful in its own way because of his personal charisma.[33]

The next day, August 13, 1952, Thornton recorded the song with members of Otis's band at the Radio Recorders Annex off Santa Monica Boulevard in Los Angeles. The studio was part of a large recording complex with a history going back to the 1920s. Otis began the day as the producer, with Leiber and Stoller in the wings. Thornton's backup band included guitarist Pete Lewis. Otis had discovered him at a talent competition at the Barrelhouse in the late 1940s.[34] Not much is known about Lewis, though most accounts characterize him as a brilliant but moody player. He performed with Otis's band until 1956 and then faded into obscurity, his career reportedly curtailed by heavy drinking. He put in a masterful performance on "Hound Dog," with a memorable solo described by one reviewer as "fluid and funky." Although his work would not end up on the final recording, Kansas City native and Los Angeles transplant Leard Bell played drums at the session. Bell was a veteran performer who started his first band as a teenager. He played with Otis for a decade beginning in 1948, and later served as bandleader for Sam Cooke. Conflicting accounts exist regarding who played bass that day. Some sources say that it was Mario Delagarde, another shadowy figure who was with Otis's group for a while and then disappeared in the late 1950s, but Otis, who was running the session, later said that Albert Winston played bass on the record.[35]

The session got off to a bit of a rocky start when, for some reason, Leard Bell had difficulty keeping the proper time. Finally, Leiber suggested that Otis, who was more familiar with the song, leave the production booth and take over on drums, which he did. "I played drums on 'Hound Dog,'" Otis later said. "Pete Lewis on guitar and Albert Winston on bass. That's all we had was three pieces." Because Otis was contracted with another label rather than Peacock, the music was credited to "Kansas City Bill and his Orchestra." With Otis on drums, Leiber and Stoller took over producing duties by default, and it all worked out. "Although we were not credited as producers," Leiber later said, "we had written the song and run the session. Listening to the playback, and how Big Mama fulfilled our dreams, we were the happiest teenagers in the United States of America." According to Stoller, they finished off the song in two takes, with the second take being the one that they used. "Two takes," he said. "The first one was great, and the second one was greater."[36]

While the songwriters might have been giddy over the recording, complications related to the writing credits developed that later led to legal action. The dispute boiled down to Otis claiming that he had co-written "Hound Dog," and Leiber and Stoller claiming that he had not. According to Otis, the original version of the song, like others that the teenagers wrote, was peppered with derogatory racial references that had to be cleaned up. Otis told journalist Johnny Orr, "Leiber and Stoller brought me the song, 'Hound Dog.' Parts of it weren't really acceptable. I didn't like that reference to chicken and watermelon, and said 'Let's get that crap out of there.'" He went on to say that, as a result of his alterations to the lyrics, he had a financial interest in "one third of the songwriting" as well as "half the publishing." When Thornton's single came out on Peacock, the label gave Leiber, Stoller, and Otis equal billing as songwriters.[37]

In a lawsuit filed in 1957, after the Elvis Presley version made the song a global phenomenon and therefore much more valuable, Otis claimed that his specific contributions to the tune were "the entire third verse and a new line in the second verse." He said that he had a contract with Leiber and Stoller that assigned him a one-third share of royalties, as well as the songwriting credit, while Leiber and Stoller stated that the songwriting credit was not part of any deal. There was also an issue involving Otis allegedly claiming that he had power of attorney for the songwriters, after which he signed their names to agreements with Don Robey. Furthermore, because Leiber and Stoller were not yet twenty-one years of age at the time, the validity of any legal arrangement that they had with Otis (or anyone else) was in question because a parent or guardian had not been part of the process. "Elvis Presley's record came out and sold six million," Otis later said, "and somebody told them that they were underage at the time [the agreements were made] and that there was a legal maneuver they could pull called 'disaffirm the contract,' and they could cut me out completely, and they did."[38]

Meanwhile, Leiber and Stoller held fast to their story that "no part of the song was written by Otis." To them, the situation illustrated the cutthroat nature of the music business, where producers, label owners, and managers often took advantage of artists. "We learned that Johnny Otis put his name on the song as a composer," Stoller later said, "and indicated to Don Robey, the label owner, that he, Johnny, had power of attorney to sign for us as well. Well, not only was Johnny not a writer of the song, he also didn't have the right to sign for us. When we saw what he was doing, we got an attorney and a new contract from Robey." The new agreement—signed by the underage songwriters' mothers—held that Leiber and Stoller alone were the sole composers of the song, but the consistently shifty Don Robey ended up diverting most of the profits from Thornton's record into his own pockets. Lion Publishing Company, which Robey owned, held the publishing copyright for the song in the names of "Don Deadric Robey and Willie Mae Thornton," although Thornton also saw little financial return on her record. Summing up the ordeal, Stoller later said, "Big Mama's 'Hound Dog' went to #1 [in the R&B charts], sold a million copies, and did nothing for our bank statements. We were getting screwed."[39]

After the courts sided with Leiber and Stoller in 1957, ruling that they were the sole composers of "Hound Dog," Johnny Otis seemed to let the issue go. According to his biographer George Lipsitz, "The decision cost Otis millions of dollars in [songwriting] royalties, but he accepted the legal decision, always expressing sincere admiration for Leiber and Stoller's extraordinary talents as songwriters." While Otis would indeed be generous in his comments about the pair in later interviews, and recognize them as the creators of "Hound Dog," it was apparent on occasion that all was not completely forgotten, or forgiven. Some of his lingering irritation bubbled to the surface in a 1970 interview, when he described the initial settlement of the matter. When asked about the controversy, he took a sarcastic shot at Leiber and Stoller, even claiming that they had not really written the hit "Kansas City," originally recorded by Little Willie Littlefield. "You know, I did get $1,300 for 'Hound Dog,' against $150,000 that I should have gotten," he told journalist Charlie Gillett. "So, I shouldn't feel too bad, because I understand that they only gave Little Willie Littlefield fifty dollars for 'Kansas City,' that *he* wrote and they *didn't* write."[40]

Regardless of who wrote the song and who ultimately profited from it, Willie Mae Thornton's recording of "Hound Dog" impressed everyone at the recording session, but Don Robey did not release the record for several months. It finally came out in early 1953, numbered Peacock 1612, with the song "Nightmare" as the B-side. Although the response was immediate, Thornton by that time was back on tour with Otis's band, and she had apparently forgotten all about the "Hound Dog" recording session. She later said that she was in an automobile on the way to a show the first time she heard the song on the radio. "I turned on the radio and heard the record," she recalled. "The man said 'Here's a record that's going nationwide, "Hound Dog" by Willie Mae Thornton.' I said 'That's me!' When we got to the theater, they were blasting it all over. That evening I sang it on the show, and everybody went for it. 'Hound Dog' just took off like a jet." By April of 1953, the song was #1 on the *Billboard* R&B charts, where it remained for seven weeks. According to industry trade publications, it was the most listened to R&B record of the year. Accounts vary widely as far as sales figures are concerned, but the record likely sold somewhere between 500,000 and 1 million copies. Almost overnight, Thornton became one of the best known R&B stars in the country, and when she returned to New York for an engagement at the Apollo, the press hailed her as "musical royalty" and "Queen of the Blues."[41]

While "Hound Dog" launched Big Mama Thornton into the American rhythm and blues stratosphere, her flight at the top was only temporary. After the record hit the charts, Don Robey added Thornton to his "Blues Consolidated Package Show" touring troupe, headlined by Peacock star Johnny Ace and including Junior Parker and Bobby "Blue" Bland. Thornton toured with Ace for months, drawing big crowds wherever they went. Notable performances included the Fourth Annual Rhythm and Blues Jubilee in Los Angeles and another run at the Apollo in New York. She continued making records but failed to replicate the success of "Hound Dog." Tragically, Johnny Ace died from an accidental self-inflicted gunshot wound between sets of a performance in Houston on Christmas Day, 1954. Thornton witnessed the event backstage and later told authorities that Ace had been waving a pistol around and pointing it at others before aiming it at himself and pulling the trigger, not realizing that a bullet was in the chamber. The event represented the beginning of a rocky period for Thornton.[42]

After Ace's death, Thornton toured on her own, still drawing crowds, but in smaller and smaller venues. She eventually had a falling out with Don Robey—predictably, over money—and left Peacock Records. She moved to California and found steady work in clubs in San Francisco and Los Angeles. Thornton could not follow up on the success of "Hound Dog," and three years after she recorded it, Elvis Presley's version became much better known, particularly to white teenagers, who represented a coveted target market for major record labels. Through many ups and downs, she soldiered on, making records and benefitting from the blues revival of the 1960s. She made two memorable appearances at the Monterey Jazz Festival, and Janis Joplin had a hit record with "Ball and Chain," a song that Thornton wrote. In the end, the success of "Hound Dog" was bittersweet for the singer. It helped make her reputation as a formidable blues belter, but it did not allow her to sustain a lucrative career over time. She later complained to an interviewer, "I got one check for $500 [for 'Hound Dog'] and never saw another. Everybody livin' in a house but me. I'm just livin'." Thornton died in Los Angeles in 1984 at the age of fifty-seven. Three years earlier she had contacted Otis about arranging her funeral should she ever pass away. "She told me to 'make it short, and make 'em smile,'" Otis later said.[43]

Chapter 3

ANSWERS and PRETENDERS

I can tell you one thing,
there's no plagiarism in "Bear Cat."

—**SAM PHILLIPS,** *Knoxville (Tenn.) Journal,* May 3, 1953

The success of "Hound Dog" did not go unnoticed in the music industry, and it triggered a predictable response from many quarters. Within weeks of the release of Thornton's record, cover versions, copies, and "answer" tunes began appearing as others rushed to cash in on the song's popularity. The practice was common, and as old as recorded music itself. Artists, managers, producers, and label owners worked quickly to release new versions of the tune in hopes of generating sales. The racial demographics of the record-buying public ultimately dictated who covered the song and when. Although African Americans were the original target market for "Hound Dog," most Black artists were hesitant to make a cover version, at least at first, because Thornton's masterpiece was so dominant in the R&B marketplace. Instead, white country and western performers came up with their own arrangements, complete with peddle steel guitars and honky-tonk pianos, and made recordings of the song designed to appeal to untapped white audiences. For the most part, these versions used the original lyrics, though no country performer could ever replicate Thornton's intensity. Early country versions of the song were not sanitized per se, but altered tempos and phrasings usually created a finished product that was more of a novelty number, flashy but far less fierce than the original. None did too well in terms of sales or earned the songwriters much in terms of royalties, but in many ways they paved the way for Elvis Presley's later take on the song.

The only significant R&B cover of "Hound Dog" released immediately in Thornton's wake was by Johnny Otis protégé "Little Esther" Phillips. By 1953, she was under contract with Federal Records, a subsidiary of King Records in Cincinnati. Otis had a hand in arranging the session, and filed a shaky copyright on the new version of the song. Backing Phillips in the studio were veteran players Rufus Gore on tenor saxophone, Hank Marr on piano, John Faire on guitar, Clarence Mack on bass, and Calvin Shields on drums. Predictably, the record went nowhere, as Little Esther simply could not compete with Big Mama in the studio, or anywhere else for that matter. The music business was unforgiving, and in R&B circles there was only room for one female blues belter's version of "Hound Dog."[1]

In the meantime, country versions came fast and furious. While several appeared at almost the same time, Billy Starr's recording of "Hound Dog" on the Imperial label was probably the first. Founded in the late 1940s, Imperial specialized in R&B and country tunes, and in 1953 it was the home of popular country and folk artist Slim Whitman. Born James William Stallard in 1913 in Wesleyville, Kentucky, Starr was a minor figure on the country music scene, but fairly well known in his home state and parts of the Midwest. He worked as a disc jockey and performed during the 1940s as "Kentucky Bill" Stallard. For a time, he also sang western songs on the radio and at live events as a character called "Indian Bill." Eventually settling on Billy Starr as a stage moniker, he appeared on the *Grand Ole Opry* during the summer of 1950 as one of the opening acts for stalwarts Ernest Tubb, Minnie Pearl, and Hank Williams. He also toured consistently with Lloyd Estel "Cowboy" Copas, the popular but doomed troubadour who perished in the same 1963 plane crash that killed Patsy Cline and Hawkshaw Hawkins.[2]

Released within a month of Thornton's classic, Billy Starr's "Hound Dog" was touted in print advertisements as "The Original Country and Western Version." The antagonist of the song was changed from a man to a woman, but otherwise it stayed mostly true to Leiber and Stoller's original lyrics. A twangy, rockabilly-style guitar and a boogie-woogie piano accented the record, with Starr ad-libbing "Get away from my door, Mama!" during the guitar solo. Referencing Thornton's hit, the April 4, 1953, edition of *Billboard* gave Starr's interpretation a decent review, stating, "The new ditty [Thornton's original], which is busting wide open in the R & B field, is sold here in a very effective and exciting style by Billy Starr, over a good combo backing. [It] should pull spins and plays in the country markets and could move out." Despite the positive press, the song never made much of an impact, though it did receive considerable airplay through the end of the year.[3]

A group of studio veterans using the name "Jack Turner and his Granger County Gang" cut a smoother country version of "Hound Dog" for RCA Victor. The musicians, all of whom already had solid careers, were part of a collective known as the Country All-Stars, led by guitarist and producer Chet Atkins. Among those in the group besides Atkins were singer Henry D. Haynes, Kenneth C. Burns on mandolin, bassist Charles Green, and Jerry Byrd on steel guitar. Other musicians came and went depending on their availability. Haynes and Burns had previously made a name for themselves on radio and in theaters as the country comedy team "Homer and Jethro." Haynes handled the vocals on this version on "Hound Dog," which was recorded in New York on March 20, 1953. The arrangement was pure country, but the song's crisp sound reflected the high production values associated with major record labels. As with Starr's version of the tune, the Ganger County Gang's rendering ended up doing little business.[4]

Intro Records, a subsidiary of Eddie and Leo Messner's Aladdin label, was responsible for a trio of 1953 country versions of "Hound Dog." Intro released North Carolinian Eddie Hazelwood's "Hound Dog" to lukewarm praise, with one reviewer calling it "an effective country blues item." A military veteran who moved to Hollywood after the Second World War, Hazelwood was a prolific songwriter whose tunes were recorded by a long list of country singers, including Johnny Bond, Johnny Horton, and Porter Wagoner. During his career, he cut more than a dozen sides for Intro and worked with other labels, though his interpretation of Big Mama Thornton's song never got much airplay. Betsy Gay's Intro version of "Hound Dog" was unique because it was the only country cover of the period sung by a woman. A former child actress who appeared in a handful of films during the 1930s and early 1940s, Gay was twenty-four when she made the record. While she was female and could, like Thornton, deliver the song from a female perspective, Gay's offering was no more successful than those of her male counterparts. Summing up shortcomings that could apply to any country retread of the Thornton single, a *Billboard* reviewer wrote, "Betsy Gay tackles the wild blues effort now creating a blaze in the R & B field. She sings it well, shouting out the lyrics with occasional excitement, though without the power the tune needs."[5]

A cover by Tommy Duncan stayed afloat on the airwaves for several months, more than likely because he had significant name recognition. Duncan was well known as one of the founding members of Bob Wills's western swing band the Texas Playboys. He was the lead vocalist on most of their hits, including "San Antonio Rose" and "Stay All Night," and appeared with the band in several films. After leaving Wills, Duncan formed his own successful group, Tommy Duncan and His Western All Stars, and also performed with the Miller Brothers Orchestra, a seasoned and very popular eight-piece dance band. With the Miller Brothers backing him up, Duncan's "Hound Dog" had a distinctive jazz feel, although most considered it a country record. This was no surprise considering Duncan's background with the Texas Playboys, who routinely combined the dance music of jazz with their traditional folk and country instruments. The Miller Brothers group was a versatile outfit known for "playing everything from the very latest tunes to the oldest hoedowns." As a result, Duncan's cover featured a moaning trumpet and other brass instruments that made the record seem a bit like a cross between Count Basie and Ernest Tubb.[6]

While it was not a cover version of "Hound Dog" with regard to lyrics, Overton Amos Lemons, known professionally as Smiley Lewis, recorded a song called "Playgirl" in March of 1953 that used a similar melody with different words. Lewis was a Louisiana native who cut his musical teeth in the French Quarter nightclubs of New Orleans. He grew up in the same neighborhood as successful bandleader, arranger, and producer Dave Bartholomew, who in 1950 invited him into the studio to record for Imperial Records. Lewis achieved moderate success in the 1950s with "The Bells Are Ringing," "One Night," and "Please Listen to Me," as well as "I Hear You Knockin'," a song that was a huge hit for Fats Domino. Lewis recorded "Playgirl" in 1953, with the writing credit going to Bartholomew. The song chronicles the laments of a man whose party-loving girlfriend has "left him in misery." The melody closely matched "Hound Dog," with the hook for the song stating that the woman "ain't nothing but a playgirl."[7]

Like cover versions, "answer songs" were a vehicle for taking advantage of—and profiting from—the popularity of an original tune. As the name implies, an answer song was written and performed in direct response to an existing record, usually appropriating at least part of the music and lyrics of the original. They were more controversial because, unlike cover versions, they often muddied the water with regard to copyrights and songwriting credits. "It's an opportunistic way to shamelessly hitch your record to a recent hit," an annoyed Jerry Leiber once said of the practice. As record companies released cover versions of "Hound Dog," they also issued answer songs to Big Mama Thornton's offering. Popular in blues and country circles from the 1920s to the 1950s, answer songs sometimes featured a female response to a male performer's record, or vise versa. For example, Midwestern vocalist Charlie Gore, with guitarist Louis Innes, recorded a country answer to "Hound Dog" titled "(You Ain't Nothin' But a Female) Hound Dog." The pair delivered the song from a male perspective, telling the story of a woman who had little to be desired as a girlfriend.[8]

While most blues artists of the period seemed hesitant to make a traditional cover of Thornton's hit, they were not shy about producing answers to it. Bluesman Roy Brown, whose 1947 hit "Good Rocking Tonight" is still considered an early rock 'n' roll classic, recorded "Mr. Hound Dog's in Town" for King. Brown delivered the song in the first person, musically casting aspersions on a female companion as he defended himself from her claims that he was a miscreant. Despite drawing heavily on Big Mama Thornton's original for melody and lyrics, Brown took the writing credit for the song, which would have probably drawn a court challenge had it been more popular. *Billboard* was impressed enough to write a positive review, complimenting the side as "mighty strong material, powerfully chanted and played," that should "capitalize on the excitement generated by the original."[9]

Louisiana bluesman Jimmie Wilson released another first-person answer on Big Town Records titled "Call Me a Hound Dog." West Coast producer Bob Geddins owned the label, and he took the writing credit for the song, which had mostly different lyrics and a beat that was somewhat different from the original although obviously an homage. *Billboard* gave the record a vanilla review, stating that Wilson sang the tune in an "okay style," and that his backing band "could have added a stronger beat." The disc never made the charts and quickly disappeared. The following year, Geddins pushed a follow-up record titled "New Hound Dog," by Frank "Dual Trumpeter" Motley and his Motley Crew, with Curley Bridges on vocals. Motley was an accomplished session man and touring musician who, as his nickname implies, was known for hoisting two instruments at a time. Curley was a road-seasoned vocalist who had sung with some of the country's leading jazz and R&B artists. "New Hound Dog" was faster paced than the original, called by some more of a "rock 'n' roll" version as opposed to a strictly blues number.[10]

Measured by the talent that played on the recording, Chess Records released perhaps the most musically formidable answer song in 1953 in the form of John Brim's "Rattlesnake." Founded in Chicago in 1950 by Phil and Leonard Chess, the label famously established itself as one of the world's great purveyors of blues music. As such, there was never a shortage of quality session players hanging around the Chess studio when the time came to make a record. Brim was a blues guitarist and tunesmith from Kentucky who recorded with several labels. His best known commercial hit, "Ice Cream Man," was popularized not by himself but by the rock band Van Halen, who in 1978 released a cover version that garnered considerable airplay. Hoping like others to take advantage of Big Mama Thornton's "Hound Dog," Leonard Chess asked Brim to pen an answer song. Brim obliged with a song that followed the basic structure of the original, with some altered words that had the singer disparaging his girlfriend as a conniving serpent rather than a wayward canine.[11]

A banner group of session musicians backed Brim on "Rattlesnake." Among them was Chess stalwart Willie Dixon on standup bass. One of the most influential bluesmen of the postwar era, Dixon personified Chicago blues, and his own writing credits included classics such as "Hoochie Coochie Man," "Little Red Rooster," and "I Just Want to Make Love to You." Harmonica virtuoso "Little Walter" Jacobs also appeared on the track, adding his distinctive sound. Jacobs had previously performed with Muddy Waters's band, and was less than a year removed from releasing his own breakthrough hit, "Juke," a harmonica instrumental that rode the top of the *Billboard* R&B

charts for several weeks. Rounding out the lineup were brothers Louis and Dave Myers on guitars and Fred Below on drums, all of whom had played on Jacobs's recordings. They were familiar faces on the Chicago club circuit and valued session players at Chess. The same cast of character appeared on the record's B-side, a slower offering titled "It Was a Dream." When the time came to print the labels for records, both sides were credited to "John Brim and His Stompers."

"Rattlesnake" was a well-produced blues record scheduled for release by Chess subsidy Checker, but in the end it was not meant to be. The Chess brothers pulled it from distribution at the last minute, spooked by potential legal challenges from Don Robey. Robey did not threaten Chess directly, but he had begun threatening others who were trying to profit from "Hound Dog." Brim's "Rattlesnake" would not be released for sixteen years, finally appearing on a 1969 Chess album titled *Whose Muddy Shoes* that featured songs by Brim and Elmore James.[12]

Trumpet player Jake Porter founded the R&B label Combo Records in 1951, and two years later joined the parade of producers hoping to cash in on "Hound Dog." He enlisted saxophonist and bandleader Chuck Higgins to record an answer song. Higgins had recently scored a regional hit on the West Coast with "Pachuko Hop," which found a significant audience in California's Hispanic community. He had played with Charlie Parker and a number of other jazz greats, and led his owned jump blues band called the Mellotones, featuring his brother Fred on vocals, as well as a young Johnny "Guitar" Watson. Higgins titled his answer song "Real Gone Hound Dog" and stuck with the formula of creating a recognizable but not exact version of the original. He took the writing credit along with Porter, who was listed on the label under the pseudonym "V. Haven." The record sold a few copies, mainly around Southern California, and Higgins routinely featured the song as part of his stage act.[13]

A duet featuring Eugene Jackson and Juanita Moore titled "You Call Me a Hound Dog" had a different spirit from other answer songs, promoting a much brighter message. It was also unusual because Jackson and Moore were accomplished actors as well as singers. Jackson began his long show business career as a child in silent films, including a notable appearance with Mary Pickford in the 1925 film *Little Annie Rooney.* He also played a character nicknamed Pineapple in an early incarnation of Hal Roach's *Our Gang* comedies. Moore studied acting in Los Angeles before moving to New York, where she appeared in plays and took part in elaborate stage shows at the famous Cotton Club in Harlem. She then returned to California and during the 1940s started a film career.

John Dolphin was the producer behind the Jackson and Moore answer song. Dolphin was a prominent member of the Los Angeles music community and one of the city's more notable characters. In 1948, on Central Avenue, he opened Dolphin's of Hollywood, a twenty-four-hour record store and general hangout spot for jazz and blues musicians. The store also hosted radio programs featuring the city's most prominent African American disc jockeys. Dolphin founded his own record label, Recorded in Hollywood, around the same time, but that effort was plagued with financial setbacks. Desperate to generate revenue, Dolphin signed Jackson and Moore in 1953 to answer Big Mama Thornton's hit. Their version was a copy of Jimmie Wilson's number, with Bob Geddins retaining the songwriting credit.

What made their song different was an alternating delivery of the lyrics—first Jackson, then Moore—which turned the recording into a conversation between a man and a woman. Rather than a monologue with one person chastising another, their effort was a give and take between affectionate parties. Jackson playfully laments that "she calls me a hound dog," with Moore responding, "You're just what I've been looking for." As a result, the song's lyrics spun a positive story of two people coming together rather than two people who are at odds. The record did not sell well, but it was the most upbeat of the period's "Hound Dog" knockoffs. As for Jackson and Moore, after the record came out, they both continued successful acting careers on television and in films, with Moore garnering an Academy Award nomination in 1959 for her performance in *Imitation of Life*.[14]

By far the most controversial answer to Big Mama Thornton's "Hound Dog" sprang from a tiny recording studio at 706 Union Avenue in Memphis, Tennessee. While the bare-bones space was compact and utterly nondescript, it would one day be globally famous. A former disc jockey and radio engineer named Sam Phillips ran the studio, and he was destined for fame as well.

Sam Phillips was born in Florence, Alabama, in 1923, the youngest in a farm family that included eight children. He picked cotton as a youngster, and as a teenager he held a number of odd jobs. As was the case with many who worked hard in rural areas during the Great Depression, Phillips often sought solace through the radio, which miraculously brought the outside world into even the most isolated home. "I was in love with sound, in love with the radio," he once said. "Radio took me away." Like other whites in the South, Phillips was exposed to African American culture on a regular basis, even though segregation was the law of the land, and from an early age African American music fascinated him. He heard African American agricultural workers singing in the fields, and sometimes he loitered outside local Black churches listening to high-energy gospel. The experiences affected the rest of his life. "I'd seen them work," he later said. "And I saw how they kept their spirituality. They felt hope, and to me that said something."[15]

In 1939, Phillips took a life-altering road trip to Texas with several friends, including his older brother J. W., who aspired to be a preacher. The group piled into a car—Phillips later remembered it as "a '37 Dodge with a rumble seat"—and left Alabama for Dallas to attend a revival meeting led by famous Southern Baptist minister George W. Truett. On the way, they passed through Memphis and drove down Beale Street, one of the richest musical avenues in the United States. The experience made a deep impression on Phillips, and afterward his life was never quite the same. "I'd heard about Beale Street. I'd heard it was the most unique street in the world," he later told an interviewer. "And we drove down Beale—it must have been five o'clock in the morning, and believe me, this street was busy. . . . We drove up and down Beale half a dozen times, and God, it was so active and vibrant and alive." Not only were the clubs going strong, but music seemed to literally be everywhere. "You had somebody on practically every corner," he said, "strumming a guitar, or playing a lard can with a broomstick and a string. I had the perception kind of like being in a religious meeting." For a carload of white kids from northern Alabama, taking a ride down Beale Street, a haven for African American entertainment, was almost like taking a trip to the moon.[16]

It was little wonder that the sounds and images of Beale Street stuck with Sam Phillips. By the late 1930s, African American culture there was in full flower. The avenue had been the heart of the African American entertainment district in Memphis for decades, and the home of nightclubs that on a regular basis hosted some of the country's greatest musicians. The area was

Memphis record producer and entrepreneur Sam Phillips. Phillips claimed a writing credit for "Bear Cat," a "Hound Dog" answer song, leading to a significant lawsuit over copyright infringement. Colin Escott/Getty Images.

much more than just an evening destination for people looking to kick up their heels. Called by many "The Main Street of Negro America," Beale Street fostered a sense of community among the area's oppressed Black population. It was a place where they could shop, socialize, and take a brief respite from the Jim Crow system that ruled their daily lives. Merchants of various types made a living on "daytime Beale," but after sunset "nighttime Beale" pulsated to a different rhythm. It attracted people from all walks of life, from community pillars to hedonists and hucksters, and the area's nightlife made Memphis the regional center of an exciting music culture. "On Saturday Beale Street is thronged with Negroes from Arkansas, northern Mississippi and western Tennessee," a WPA writer recorded in the 1930s. "Though quiet and peaceful in daytime, [at night] streetwalkers and guitar players stroll up and down the avenue. . . . From pianos in crowded honkytonks comes the slow hesitation beat of the blues, or the furious stomp of swing music." In his 1934 book *Beale Street: Where the Blues Began,* African American business executive and political leader George W. Lee wrote that while Beale was peaceful during the day, "when the sun sinks into the river and the stars come out, it sings, laughs, drinks and dances until early morning."[17]

After the Second World War, blues musicians provided much of Beale Street's soundtrack as guitarists and singers flocked to Memphis in hopes of landing engagements in the clubs. Composer and bandleader W. C. Handy, who helped put Memphis on the map as a blues mecca, later described the music played on Beale as "the sounds of the sinner on revival day!" The process of playing music also began to change after the war, as electric amplification of both instruments and voices came into widespread use. Like their counterparts in Chicago, New Orleans, St. Louis, and elsewhere, the musicians on Beale "plugged in" to deliver an older form of music in a new, more explosive way. Among those seeking to better their fortunes in Memphis was B. B. King. Born into a poor family as Riley King in northern Mississippi, he traveled across the state line into Tennessee after the war and began a career that made him an international star. For King, and people like him, Beale Street was a musical land of milk and honey. "When I first came to Memphis, Beale Street was very active," he later recalled. "Many little clubs on Beale Street, with music going on all up and down the street on the weekend. . . . Even guys with names would come and play or listen to people play." Booker "Bukka" White, another Mississippi musician who ended up in Memphis after the war, summed up the atmosphere more succinctly when he once told an interviewer, "If there ever was a good time, so help me God, there was good times on Beale Street."[18]

As musicians flocked to the city, postwar Memphis also experienced the further rise of radio as an entertainment medium, and one station in particular helped revolutionize the musical reputation of the city. WDIA entered the Memphis radio market with its first broadcast on June 7, 1947. Founded by white owners John R. Pepper and Bert Ferguson, it was the sixth station to begin operation in Memphis, and boasted "a 380 foot antenna located about two miles from the studios at 2074 Union Avenue." Despite a good deal of promotion, the station got off to a sluggish start, programming a benign jumble of classical, country, and pop standards that drew few listeners. Tired of losing money, Pepper and Ferguson made the decision to tap into the previously ignored African American market in Memphis, which included around 40 percent of the city's population.[19]

It was a risky proposition for a white-owned radio station to aggressively court Black listeners in the Jim Crow South of the 1940s, but a dollar was still a dollar, so the owners took the gamble and it paid off. They hired Nat D. Williams, billed as "the South's first Negro disc jockey," to host an African American music program called *Tan Town Jamboree* that premiered on October 28, 1948. The show featured blues and R&B music, with a little gospel thrown in for good measure. At the time, it was a playlist not usually featured on the radio. "We came up with the idea of giving [the audience] some blues," Williams later recalled, "but the only Black record we had at the station was 'Stompin' at the Savoy,' and it was by a white writer. We started scrounging around and finally got some records by some blues artists like Fats Waller and Ivory Joe Turner. . . . First thing you know it caught on. The listeners were ready for a new sound, it seemed."[20]

Tan Town Jamboree was a hit, and within a year WDIA had an "all-Black" format featuring more Black disc jockeys. Williams became "the Voice of Beale Street" and the most recognizable African American entertainment figure in Memphis. Most of Memphis's Black population began listening to WDIA on a regular basis, where they heard for the first time music, news, advertisements, and public affairs programs geared toward their specific wants and needs. It was a situation that they had never encountered before. "There's a radio revolution going on here in Memphis," Williams wrote at the time in a column for the *Pittsburgh (Pa.) Courier,* an African American newspaper. "It's the talk of the town. Beale Streeters from 'way back' are taking note of the situation and making notes as to how things are developing."

The success of WDIA led stations in other cities to court African American listeners and devote more and more time to African American performers. In addition to creating more opportunities for Black entertainers, this had social implications that would help determine the future of American music. "When I left my home in Indianola [Mississippi]," B. B. King said, "every time I heard something about a black person, it was when they did something wrong. It was never praising them. Rarely would you hear of anything positive being done by a black person. WDIA was a light."[21]

In 1953, WDIA successfully applied to increase its signal to a robust 50,000 watts, meaning that its broadcasts could escape the Memphis area. It was a big step destined to bring the station a huge number of new listeners. Nat D. Williams knew it was a turning point, and opined "[WDIA's] programs, beamed for the Negro market, will be covering an area stretching from the Mason-Dixon line on the north, to the Gulf of Mexico heading south . . . from Ol' Man River going east to the foothills of Nashville, from the mighty Mississippi heading west to the Ozarks. More than one-tenth of the nation's Negroes will be reached by WDIA's dial number." The station officially made the leap in 1954 and began beaming "50,000 watts of goodwill" throughout the Southeast, increasing both its influence and its legend. Suddenly, it was possible for local radio performers to become known outside of the immediate confines of Memphis, and the sales of records broadcast on WDIA increased dramatically. The station still played music, but now it could help launch careers.[22]

In Memphis and throughout the South, more and more African American music was broadcast over the airwaves, but it was not to an exclusively Black audience. Some whites listened to the growing number of Black stations, gaining an appreciation for African American music that would alter the musical marketplace. When asked later, some of the earliest African American disc jockeys estimated that as much as half of their audience may have been white. The free spirit of youth led many white teenagers to the altar of blues and R&B, where some began worshiping freely. Prior to the emergence of Black radio, music in the South was as segregated as the rest of Jim Crow society. Most whites were not exposed to blues music to any great degree, but commercial radio changed the entertainment landscape. The airwaves belonged to everyone, regardless of race, and as a result WDIA and stations like it provided an integrated soundtrack for the lives of those who were willing to listen. It was a transformative development in American culture that resonated from that point forward.[23]

Meanwhile, Sam Phillips never forgot his first trip down Beale Street. He and his friends returned to Florence after their sojourn to Texas, and Phillips worked a variety of odd jobs, including delivering bread and driving a hearse to pick up bodies for a funeral home. While still in high school he started a dance band, and the group's appearance on a local radio program led to his first significant radio job as a record spinner at WMSD (later WLAY) in nearby Sheffield, Alabama. It paid very little but got his foot in the door as a local broadcaster. He entertained notions of one day becoming a lawyer, but when his father died in 1941 he quit school to help support his family. More radio jobs followed. There was a stint at WMSL in Decatur, Alabama, and even a part-time job at powerful WLAC in Nashville. A friend told Phillips about an opening at WREC in Memphis, and Sam jumped at the opportunity to begin what he considered at the time to be a dream job. He moved his family to Memphis and started work at the station, announcing, engineering, and supervising nightly big band broadcasts from the rooftop ballroom of the Peabody Hotel. It was the beginning of an entertainment career that eventually made him a cultural icon in the city, and one of the most well-known Memphians in the world. "Memphis represented something wonderful," his wife, Becky, later told an interviewer. "Memphis was the world to him."[24]

While Phillips enjoyed his job at the station, he also nurtured another dream. He wanted to open his own recording studio, where he hoped to record Black artists and market the music to both African Americans and whites, a bold proposition at the time. "I was fascinated by doing what I was doing with the big bands," he later said. "But, I had heard the innate rhythms of Beale Street—the blues, the blues, the blues." He believed in the project and drew some inspiration from WDIA's recent conversion to an all-Black format. He opened the Memphis Recording Service in January of 1950 at 706 Union Avenue and printed business cards stating that he would record "anything, anywhere, at any time." It took about a year of recording weddings, recitals, and civic events just to stay afloat before he was able to turn his full attention to producing African American musicians like Ike Turner, Howlin' Wolf, and B. B. King. "I wasn't in it just to record black music for black people alone," he told an interviewer years later. "I was in it to record something I loved, something I felt, something I thought other people ought to have an opportunity to render judgement on. And most especially young whites [and] young blacks."[25]

What Phillips was doing in Memphis was groundbreaking, but it was not particularly profitable, at least in the beginning. Only so many community events needed his services, and the slow parade of amateurs he recorded did little to help his bottom line. Eventually things picked up and Phillips made a number of recordings of African American artists that he sold or leased to labels like Chess in Chicago and RPM, a subsidiary of Modern Records in Los Angeles. In 1952, he formed his own label, Sun Records, which also operated out of the Union Avenue office in Memphis. "I truly did not want to open a record label," he later claimed, "but I was forced into it by those labels either coming to Memphis to record or taking my artists elsewhere. Sun Records was forced on me, but at the same time, it presented the opportunity to do exactly what I wanted." Among the first artists to record for the new label were saxophonist Johnny London, Walter Bradford and the Big City Four, Handy Jackson, and Joe Hill Louis, none of whose work sold well. But in early 1953, Phillips recorded local African American disc jockey Rufus Thomas, whose voice and personality helped produce Sun's first hit.[26]

Rufus C. Thomas Jr. was born to sharecropping parents in Marshall County, Mississippi, on March 26, 1917. On the eve of the Great Depression, his family moved to Memphis, where he grew up participating in school-sponsored shows and tap dancing on the streets for nickels and dimes. By the time he was a teenager it was obvious that Thomas was a natural showman. He performed comedy routines in the clubs and theaters on Beale Street, and his outgoing spirit made him popular with audiences. He later toured the country with the Rabbit Foot Minstrels tent show. "I was with the Rabbits Foot Minstrels, but actually it was vaudeville, that's all," he later remembered. "I was a very good tap dancer. . . . we had chorus girls, comedians, dancers, and I was on there as a tap dancer." Afterward, he returned to settle in Memphis and pursue an entertainment career. He became a fixture on Beale Street and hosted a weekly amateur talent show at the Palace Theater that gave well-know artists like B. B. King and Bobby "Blue" Bland some of their first exposures. Thomas's act was a mix of quick-witted comedy ban-

Popular Memphis entertainment personality Rufus Thomas, who was the lead vocalist on "Bear Cat." Special Collections Department, University of Memphis Libraries.

ter and music, but it was his happily extroverted personality that audiences adored. "I was on stage long before I started doing radio," he later said. "I worked mostly local nightclubs in Memphis, but there was one theater show every week, 'Amateur Night on Beale Street,' at the Palace Theater. Everybody used to come and do the show. . . . I did that job for eleven years."[27]

Thomas became one of Beale Street's most prominent personalities, which led to a job at WDIA not long after the station switched to an all African American format. Nat D. Williams, who was a mentor to the young entertainer, hired him as a disc jockey and general on-air personality. On Thomas's shows, he played records by artists ranging from the established to the unknown, and did his best to promote local talent. Unfortunately for Thomas, his popularity did not generate enough income to consistently feed his family, so he also worked a day job in a Memphis textile mill. Every weekday at the mill began at 6:30 a.m. and ended mid-afternoon, just in time to make it to the studio for his shift. "I'd finish [at the mill] at two-thirty, run home, go to the station, and be on the air at three o'clock. I did that for years and years. I also did weekend live shows, and often I'd get home at four o'clock on Monday morning and be punching a clock at six-thirty." The fact that Thomas was able to maintain that schedule for years was a testament to the energy and attitude that made him a star in Memphis. While he never fancied himself as a true singer, Thomas began a recording career in the early 1950s. Some people said he looked a little like Louis Armstrong, but his delivery was more like Louis Jordan, fast-paced and fun.[28]

It was inevitable that Thomas would cross paths with Sam Phillips. Both men loved Beale Street, albeit from different perspectives, and both were interested in promoting Black talent. Thomas knew everyone on the avenue and was plugged in to the Memphis music scene, while Phillips admired the musicians there and wanted to record them. At the time, many smaller labels liked making singers out of disc jockeys, recording and promoting those who had talent. The practice created a bond between the label and the radio station where the disc jockeys worked, guaranteeing that songs the label produced would receive airplay. In June of 1951, Phillips recorded Thomas and leased three songs to Chess Records. They received little attention, but two years later, after opening Sun, he thought about Thomas again.[29]

Big Mama Thornton's "Hound Dog" caught Phillips's ear when it came out in early 1953, causing him—like many others—to ponder how he might capitalize on the song's success. Covers and answers to the song appeared almost immediately after Peacock released the original, and Phillips jumped on the bandwagon. Not wanting to produce another artist singing a straight cover, he envisioned an answer song with a creative "hook" to catch the public's attention. With Thornton's recording, listeners heard a strong-willed woman with threadbare patience chastise a Lothario. After giving it some thought, Phillips came up with the idea to reverse the roles. Rather than a woman berating a man, he liked the premise of a male protagonist scolding an overbearing woman. He wrote some new lyrics on the fly, and turned "Hound Dog" into "Bear Cat," which was a slang term for an outgoing or "wild" woman. Phillips kept the same melody as the Leiber and Stoller hit, but the signature line in his song was "You ain't nothin' but a bear cat," followed by the altered words.[30]

There was a comedic undertone to "Bear Cat" that was probably what led Phillips to believe Rufus Thomas was the right person to record it. Thomas came into the studio and Phillips pitched him the idea. At first, Thomas, who was not familiar with the term *bear cat,* was skeptical. He did not really understand the dynamics of the tune until Phillips explained, "Rufus, hell, you don't know what a damn bear cat is? That's the meanest goddamn woman in the world." Thomas was also not enamored with the band that Phillips put together. Thomas believed that his style was a better fit for musicians who played up-tempo, "jump blues" with a more sophisticated sound. Phillips instead put together a tight unit that he used frequently to record more basic country blues with "driving rhythms and scorching, distorted solos." Thomas saw himself coming from more of a Louis Jordan mold, while Phillips's players, including guitarist Joe Hill Louis, bassist Tuff Green, and drummer Houston Stokes, were comfortable backing the likes of Howlin' Wolf.[31]

Thomas and the musicians assembled to make the record at the Sun studio in Memphis on March 8, 1953. True to his vaudeville roots, and as a reflection of his own showmanship, Thomas begins "Bear Cat" with an imitation of an agitated cat, and then engages in loud, introductory banter, scolding a woman who has worn out her welcome with him. In the middle of the number, Joe Hill Louis launches into a long guitar solo, and at the end Thomas punctuates the record with more cat sounds. The final product was a recording that was more fun than the original "Hound Dog," but with a good bit less grit and grind. It was more of a novelty number than a solid blues statement, but it was definitely entertaining. The B-side was a slow, "melancholy blues effort" titled "Walking in the Rain." When Phillips had the record pressed, each 45 rpm copy carried the label "Bear Cat," accompanied with a parenthetical "(The Answer to Hound Dog)." The label also referred to Thomas as "Rufus HOUND DOG Thomas, Jr.," in an attempt to further capitalize on Big Mama Thornton's original offering.[32]

Whether it was Thomas's delivery, or the band's musicianship, or simply the fact that "Bear Cat" sounded so much like "Hound Dog," Phillips quickly found himself with a hit on his hands. One of the record's first printed reviews called it "a good disk [that] should be a coin-grabber." Less than a month after Peacock released the original, Sun released Thomas's answer song, and it had a meteoric rise up the *Billboard* charts. "It used to be that the answers to hits waited until the hit had started on a downward trail," the magazine reported on March 28, 1953, "but today the answers are ready a few days after [the original] records start moving upward." As "Hound Dog" topped the national R&B charts, "Bear Cat" crept into the regional listings. By April 11 it was #2 on the charts in New Orleans, and #10 in Atlanta and St. Louis. It made its debut in the national R&B charts as a best seller that same week at #9. "Bear Cat" stayed in the national listings for most of the month of May—seven weeks altogether—peaking at #3, two spots behind "Hound Dog." It was the first hit produced by Sun, but instead of representing a positive turning point for his label, the record's success got Sam Phillips in trouble.[33]

Don Robey was among those who noticed "Bear Cat" rising up the charts, and his response was immediate. After hearing the record, he was angry because it sounded so much like "Hound Dog," and because the label listed Phillips as sole composer of the tune. At the time, the legal framework of R&B music publishing was fluid. Artists freely borrowed lyrics that were assumed to be in the public domain, and many successful records spawned covers, copies, and answer tunes that were sometimes difficult to distinguish from one another in the context of who might deserve royalties. Conflict over money between composers, publishers, and performers was frequent, as the courts had not yet generated enough legal precedents to clearly define some of the murkier aspects of the record business. Of course, none of that mattered to Robey, who was firm in his belief that "Bear Cat" was a copy of "Hound Dog," and that Sam Phillips was a music thief. The fact that "Bear Cat" was a hit, and therefore a profitable recording, only amplified Robey's desire to do something about the situation.

National Best Sellers

Records are ranked in order of their current national selling importance at the retail level. Results are based on The Billboard's weekly survey among dealers thruout the country with a high volume of sales in rhythm and blues records. The reverse side of each record is also listed.

This Week		Last Week	Weeks on Chart
1.	HOUND DOG—W. M. Thornton Night Mare—Peacock 1612—BMI	1	5
2.	(MAMA) HE TREATS YOUR DAUGHTER MEAN—Ruth Brown R. B. Blues—Atlantic 986—ASCAP	2	14
3.	BEAR CAT—R. Thomas Jr. Walkin' in the Rain—Sun 181—BMI	9	2
4.	CRAWLIN'—The Clovers Yes, It's You—Atlantic 989	3	7
5.	LET ME GO HOME WHISKEY—A. Milburn Three Times a [illegible]—Aladdin 3161—BMI	5	9
6.	I WANNA KNOW—Du Droppers Laughing Blues—[illegible]20-5229; (45)47-5229—BMI	10	2
7.	RED TOP—King Pleasure Jumpin' With Symphony Sid—Prestige 821—BMI	4	4
8.	WOKE UP THIS MORNING—B. B. King Don't Have to Cry—RPM 380—BMI	6	5
9.	GOIN' TO THE RIVER—Fats Domino Going to the Mardi Gras—Imperial 5231—BMI	—	1
10.	BABY, DON'T DO IT—Five Royales Take All of Me—Apollo 443—BMI	7	11

Billboard magazine's R&B chart of "National Best Sellers" for the week of April 25, 1953, showing "Hound Dog" at #1 and "Bear Cat" at #3. Author's collection.

Robey took swift action against the Memphis outfit. The first step was sending a licensing agreement to Sun allowing for a standard 2-cent-per-record royalty to be paid to Lion Publishing Company. Predictably, Phillips ignored the notice and kept pressing "Bear Cat," at which point Robey threatened to sue. "I hope this will not cause any unfriendly relations," Robey wrote to Phillips in an April 4, 1953, communication, "but please remember, I have to pay when I intrude upon the rights of others, and certainly must protect my own rights." Robey called "Bear Cat" an "exact copy" of "Hound Dog" and warned Phillips that Sun should have secured the proper permissions before issuing the record. Phillips continued to ignore Robey's requests, and within a month the case went to court. "A crazy 'Hound Dog' and a real gone 'Bear Cat' battled it out yesterday in the juke joints of celebrated

Beale Street and in a court of law," a Memphis correspondent reported. "The Lion Publishing Company of Houston, Texas has sued the recorders of 'Bear Cat' for royalties and treble damages on the grounds that the lament is a dead steal from the recording of 'Hound Dog.'"[34]

Robey alleged that the Sun offering was a "conscious imitation." He said that it copied both the tune and many of the lyrics of the Thornton original "with only minor variations," and it would be hard for anyone listening to "Bear Cat" to disagree. Phillips tried to spin things his way, but he did not have much ground to stand on. He argued that his tune's driving, twelve-bar blues was standard to many blues numbers, and emphasized the differences in his song's lyrics. "There's a lot of differences in the words," he maintained. "This woman is calling this man 'Hound Dog.' The man didn't want to take that lying down. Our story is based on [the man] answering the woman. . . . I can tell you one thing, there's no plagiarism in 'Bear Cat.'" Despite Phillips's assertions, the writing was on the wall once the case went to court, and he had to give in, reaching an out-of-court settlement. According to published reports, Sun paid Lion around $2,000 and "agreed to pay 'Hound Dog' owners two cents per record for 79,000 waxings of 'Bear Cat' already sold and two cents a record for future sales." Phillip was also on the hook for legal fees, leaving Sun in financial disarray. "Bear Cat" may have been the Memphis label's first big hit, but it came at a high cost.[35]

The dispute between Robey and Phillips seemed to open the doors for further legal action involving Lion Publishing and the original version of "Hound Dog." Johnny Otis, who claimed co-authorship of the song, got involved through his company, Valjo Music Publishing, which was associated with King Records. Syd Nathan, the hardnosed head of King, claimed that Lion owed his company half the publishing royalties on "Hound Dog" because of King's relationship with Otis. "Copyright controversy over 'Hound Dog' has flared up anew," *Billboard* reported in August of 1953, "with King record topper, Syd Nathan, injecting himself into the hassle and demanding 50 per cent of the publisher's share." The basis of the suit was that King, through Valjo, had Otis under contract at the time that Otis claimed he helped Leiber and Stoller pen "Hound Dog" and, as a result, King was due a big piece of the financial pie generated by the song. Determined not to pay King, Nathan, Otis, or anyone else a penny, Robey threatened a separate suit against King and Valjo over Little Ether's cover of the original, as well as Roy Brown's answer song. In the end, Robey won the suit, but Otis would make another unsuccessful stab at garnering "Hound Dog" royalties four years later, after Elvis Presley made it an even more valuable commodity.[36]

Don Robey's fierce protection of the "Hound Dog" copyright, and the litigation it generated, helped alter the music publishing world. From that point forward, answer tunes and cover versions of original material were scrutinized more closely. Fewer answer songs appeared, and some companies recalled those that were already on the market. Chess Records, for instance, stopped pressing John Brim's "Rattlesnake" after Robey's altercation with Sun in hopes of avoiding any sort of financial liability. "Up to this time," one columnist reported, "R&B firms had used one another's material with impunity. . . . However, since the 'Hound Dog' decision, few record firms have attempted to answer smash hits by other companies by using the same tune with different lyrics." While Robey was naturally combative, the lawsuit against Phillips was also a sign of the times. By the 1950s, blues and R&B music had begun a slow but steady creep toward the mainstream of American culture, and the emergence of rock 'n' roll would soon accelerate that process. This made music by African American artists more valuable, and therefore something that was worth fighting for in court. While music had always been an art form, it was evolving into a very big business, and Robey's lawsuit against Sun would certainly not be the last court action related to copyright. According to an April 4, 1954, article in *Billboard,* "It is likely that with the R&B field becoming of such importance to pop publishers, some clarification of the problems [related to publishing] will be forthcoming as a result of litigation and disputes now shaping up." Phillips even garnered a measure of revenge a few months later when he prevailed in court in a contract dispute with Robey related to Sun recording artist Junior Parker.[37]

After the "Bear Cat" fiasco, Phillips took Sun Records in another direction. The catalyst for the move was a nineteen-year-old truck driver from Tupelo, Mississippi, who famously wandered into the Sun studio one day not long after Phillips had settled the lawsuit. His name was Elvis Presley and he was destined for stardom on an unprecedented level. He was white, but he effortlessly sang and moved like many of the African American artists who were working at Sun. Phillips saw dollar signs, and suddenly backed off the

Black artists he had been recording in favor of Presley and a string of other white, soon-to-be-famous "rockabilly" performers, including Jerry Lee Lewis, Carl Perkins, and Johnny Cash. Phillips recorded much of their earliest work, cementing in the minds of many his status as a founding father of rock 'n' roll. Ironically, after Presley left Sun for greener pastures, he recorded his own massively successful version of "Hound Dog," the same song that had almost bankrupted the label. Phillips held on to Sun until 1969, when he sold it to producer Shelby Singleton, but the original studio on Union Avenue in Memphis remains hallowed ground to rock fans today. Phillips died in 2003, but through the years he sat for many interviews pontificating about his life and times. Questioned mostly about his work with Presley and other music pioneers, he was occasionally asked about "Bear Cat." Although he claimed at the time of his spat with Robey that there was "no plagiarism" associated with the song, years later Phillips told music journalist Robert Palmer, "I should have known better. The melody was exactly the same as theirs, and we claimed credit for writing the damn thing."[38]

Rufus Thomas also survived "Bear Cat" intact, and went on to have a successful entertainment career, although it was not with Sun. Despite the success of the answer song, he was among the African American artists that Phillips let go after Presley arrived on the scene. Thomas was never enamored with "Bear Cat" to begin with, and he never quite got over the sting of Sun dropping him. It was a two-fold grudge. The snub denied him some professional opportunities, and in a deeper sense he believed that it was a slap in the face to all the African American artists that had recorded for the Memphis label. "When Sam picked up Elvis, he discarded everybody on the label who was black," Thomas later said. "Even before Elvis became real popular, he dropped us all. I gave him his first hit, and all the while he was looking for a white boy who could do what I could." Phillips fielded criticism for the move all his life, and always maintained that it was a business decision. "There were a number of very good R&B labels, [but] the base wasn't broad enough because of racial prejudice," he later explained. "It wasn't broad enough to get the amount of commercial airplay or general acceptance overall." In short, Phillips did what any businessman does, he followed the money, and while the racial considerations related to his decision were certainly relevant, it should be noted that there were other Black artists who did not seem to hold the move against him. “When they accuse me [of abandoning the black artists],” Phillips said years later, “you know what I tell them? I say none of their business in the first place, and in the second place there are people making black records as good as or better than I made.” Thomas apparently held no similar grudge against Presley himself, later claiming to be the first person to play one of the singer’s records on WDIA. “He was good for the industry,” Thomas later said. “He generated an interest that black artists hadn’t been able to do.”[39]

After Thomas left Sun, he had a string of successful recordings with Stax Records in Memphis during the 1960s and 1970s. Among them were popular numbers like “Do the Funky Chicken,” “(Do the) Push and Pull,” “The Breakdown,” and “Walking the Dog,” which the Rolling Stones covered on one of their early records. He continued recording and touring for years, and maintained a radio show on WDIA. Next to Elvis Presley (or perhaps in tandem with him), Thomas became Memphis’s most beloved entertainer, and a unique ambassador for the city. He died in 2001 at the age of eighty-four. Memphis and elsewhere mourned his passing, and his obituary in the *New York Times* lauded the entertainer as the “Patriarch of Memphis Soul.”[40]

By the end of 1953, “Hound Dog” had seemingly exhausted its musical life span as a contemporary recording. It had been an interesting run. Composed by two white teenagers for an African American woman, it had come and gone from the R&B charts, been covered and answered by African American blues artists as well as a string of white country players, and generated precedent-setting lawsuits. The cast of characters associated with its creation, production, and commercial distribution was wide and varied, including prolific songwriters Leiber and Stoller, blues queen Big Mama Thornton, legendary bandleader Johnny Otis, tough-as-they-come producer and promoter Don Robey, R&B pioneer Rufus Thomas, and Sam Phillips, who was destined to become a legend in rock ’n’ roll circles. As the song faded from the charts, no one could have imagined that its life span as a relevant recording was only beginning. “Hound Dog” was about to soar to new heights and be transformed from a song into a phenomenon that would overshadow everything that took place during the tune’s early existence.

Chapter 4

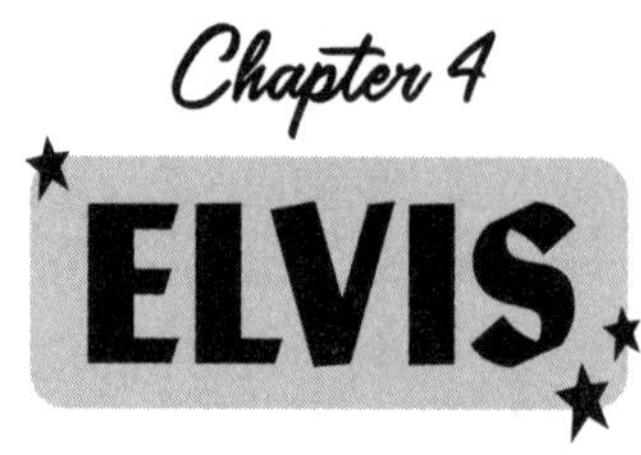

A lot of people think I started this business, but rock 'n' roll was here long before I came along. Nobody can sing that kind of music like colored people. Let's face it.

—ELVIS PRESLEY, *Jet,* August 1, 1957

A rapid musical evolution took place in the United States during the 1950s. Foundational African American blues combined with a healthy dose of white country music, and a pinch of Black and white gospel, to create a great hybrid (or what some would call a great bastard) that young people loved and their parents hated. Fans and the press called it rock 'n' roll, and it represented a musical tidal wave that changed American life forever. Scholars have attempted to dissect the elements that made early rock 'n' roll so appealing, but the job has always been difficult. The music was originally designed to be felt in the moment, and not scrutinized over the long term. Early rock 'n' roll, with its blues roots, evoked feelings in the young that did not immediately lend themselves to deep discussions about style and substance. It was new, fun, and characterized by an infectious, frantic spontaneity.

Prior to the 1950s, blues music in the United States was popular in the Black community, and with a relatively small number of whites, but the blues-based rock 'n' roll of the 1950s brought music based in the African American community to the mass of white teenagers, creating innumerable social and generational tensions in the process. To teenagers, rock 'n' roll was edgy and intoxicating, but to many older people it seemed dangerous. Many white parents were not comfortable with their sons—and especially their daughters—listening and dancing to music that was Black at its core, and peppered with sexual innuendo. This tension affected politics in the South and elsewhere during the period, as the same authorities who fought to tame rock 'n' roll also sought to check the advance of African American civil rights. Events surrounding the landmark Supreme Court desegregation case *Brown v. Board of Education of Topeka* (1954) and the rise of rock 'n' roll music happened at the same time. Both events brought Black and white young people closer together in abrupt and unprecedented ways, and rock 'n' roll music in a sense began integrating American society before much of society was ready for the change.[1] By the mid-1950s, rock 'n' roll was already drowning out the echoes of Tin Pan Alley, big band, and other forms of popular music, signaling the great shift in popular musical tastes among the young. Many teenagers and young adults embraced rock 'n' roll, the blues roots of which had been lurking in the shadows for years. The music was exciting to many, threatening to some, and sinful to others, but as a cultural phenomenon it was unstoppable.

"Hound Dog" made the transition from R&B chart topper to rock 'n' roll standard in a relatively short time, but the journey was far from seamless. Once Big Mama Thornton's rendering hit the marketplace, Black and white artists covered and copied the song almost to death in hopes of cashing in. Blues, R&B, and country versions all hit the airwaves, but none captured the success of the original. The song generated feuds and lawsuits over copyrights and publishing credits as record executives and promoters competed for every penny that Thornton's version generated. Ironically, all of this turmoil took place before "Hound Dog" became an anthem forever associated with one of the most famous entertainers in history. In the end, "Hound Dog" emerged as one of the most memorable rock 'n' roll songs of all time, but only after navigating a musical pathway accidentally cleared by a performer who often is left out of the "Hound Dog" tale. His name was Freddie Bell, and he led an early white rock 'n' roll band called Freddie Bell and the Bellboys.[2]

The son of an Italian immigrant, Freddie Bell was born Ferdinando Dominick Bello in Philadelphia on September 19, 1931, and attended South Philadelphia High School, where he had an early interest in music. He sang, played trombone and tuba in the school band, and was a proficient bass player and drummer. He joined his first band as a teenager, appearing at local dances and parties. In the 1950s, he changed his name to Freddie Bell and put together his own outfit. Bell sang and led the group, which included friends Jack Kane on saxophone, Frankie Brent on bass, Ron Conti on piano, Chick Keeney on drums, and Jerry Mayo on trumpet. The band played an eclectic mix of music that included a few R&B and "jump blues" numbers. They accented their shows with what Bell later called "showmanship," which amounted to light comedy banter and primitive choreography. Some newspaper ads described their presentation as a mixture of "vocals, comedy and jive." It was a lively show that caught on in Philadelphia. The band called themselves Freddie Bell and the Bellboys, reportedly at the suggestion of Bell's wife. "All these guys were good looking guys. Italian boys from south Philadelphia," she later recalled. "[Freddie] was funny. He could dance. He could sing and do impressions. . . . They did rock 'n' roll, standards, and everything."[3]

During the early 1950s, Bell and his cohorts made the rounds in the Philadelphia nightclubs and toured the Midwest. For a while, they landed in St. Louis, where they performed regularly at a somewhat notorious nightclub called The Terrace, across the Mississippi River in East St. Louis, Illinois. Their show offered a little bit of everything, different types of music laced with crisp dance steps and intentional buffoonery to the point that promoters sometimes billed them as a novelty act. "I was never really a rock and roller," Bell later said. "I had always been a nightclub performer. . . . We had red outfits and little bellboy caps and brass buttons. We were more of a nightclub act than a rock and roll band." The group had a tight sound, honed by constant work. They headlined in small clubs and sometimes opened for more established acts in larger venues. The group's popularity was based on their natural talent, the fast-paced but unassuming presentation of their stage show, and the fact that their repertoire was large and varied. "Freddie Bell and the Bellboys have developed their insane antics to a high point of perfection," one reviewer noted. "Bell himself fronts the group with consummate ease. . . . Their good humor on stage is extremely infectious, and they never fail to 'warm' any type of audience."[4]

As Freddie Bell and the Bellboys gained a following, they caught the attention of Bernie Lowe, a Julliard-trained pianist, bandleader, and arranger who saw great potential in the rapidly expanding teenage record market of the mid-1950s. Born Bernie Lowenthal in Philadelphia in 1917, Lowe toured

Las Vegas performers Freddie Bell and the Bellboys. Their parody version of "Hound Dog" led Elvis Presley to record his own version of the song. Micheal Ochs Archives/Getty Images.

with several orchestras before landing a job in his hometown in 1949 as musical director for *Paul Whiteman's TV Teen Club*. Hosted by jazz musician and bandleader Paul Whiteman, the show was a music and dance program catering to teenagers and featuring young performers and celebrity talent judges. A reflection of the times, its success was an early indicator that major media and media advertisers were about to take very seriously the growing teen market for entertainment and entertainment-related merchandise. *TV*

Teen Club was first broadcast from WFIL in Philadelphia on April 2, 1949, at 9:00 p.m. from a large armory building on the corner of Broad and Callowhill Streets. "Kids used to line up for tickets for that show, and pack the armory," Tom Hass, WFIL's program director, later recalled. "We did all the shows from the armory. With the size of the place, [Whiteman] could accommodate more people." Almost immediately picked up by the ABC television network, the show was seen live in the Northeast, with kinescope recordings sent for broadcast in some of the larger cities of the Midwest. Within a couple of years technology advanced to the point where true national broadcasts became possible, and ABC made *TV Teen Club* part of its prime time lineup. The show had a successful five-year run, and was a precursor to Dick Clark's Philadelphia-based *American Bandstand.*[5]

Hoping to capitalize on the growing teen music market, Lowe founded Teen Records in Philadelphia in 1954 and started looking for local acts to make the label's first recordings. Freddie Bell and the Bellboys were well known in the city, and through their touring had a regional reputation. Lowe chose them to help launch his new enterprise. Apparently familiar with either Big Mama Thornton's original "Hound Dog," or one of the many covers or answers, Lowe approached Bell about recording a new version. According to most sources, Lowe wanted to clean up the song's original wording to make it more palatable for polite society, and particularly for white, middle-class parents whose teenagers might want to purchase the record. To satisfy Lowe, Bell rewrote some of the lyrics, changing suggestive phrases like "you can wag your tail, but I ain't gonna feed you no more" to "you ain't never caught a rabbit, and you ain't no friend of mine." The finished product was indeed more "pop-friendly," but according to Jerry Leiber and Mike Stoller the new lyrics took the heart and meaning out of the song, as did a change in tempo. It also made the song somewhat nonsensical, turning it from a powerful female statement on male sloth and infidelity into an upbeat tune about a mutt. Jerry Leiber later said that Bell's version was "too fast, a nervous, 'okeedokee' cracker version that reminded me of Lonnie Donnegan, the skiffle guy popular in England at the time." Likewise, Stoller told an interviewer that Freddie Bell's retooling had "distorted" the song, taking away the rough edges that Thornton had given the original. "She was singing to a man," he said with a chuckle. "And he was singing to a dog."[6]

Freddie Bell and the Bellboys recorded their version of "Hound Dog" in 1954, and by November of that year newspaper ads for their personal appearances were billing the group as "recording stars of 'Hound Dog.'" Their version differed a good bit from the original. They changed the tempo and substituted some of Bell's new, more benign lyrics, but the writing credit on the single's label still read "Leiber and Stoller." The Bellboys version also opened with a raucous blast from a saxophone and included a healthy sax solo about midway through. While the record did not make an impact nationally, it sold well in the Philadelphia area and on the East Coast in general. As the group continued to tour, "Hound Dog" was one of the highlights of their stage act, although Bell himself did not consider it a true rock 'n' roll number. "We did some pure rock 'n' roll but there was choreography and a show around us," he later said. "If I had done pure 50s rock 'n' roll without the choreography and without the salesmanship, it wouldn't have worked." Their stage presentation of "Hound Dog" included a good bit of dancing and clowning around, which audiences seemed to like. It was definitely a novelty number for the Bellboys, both as a record and on stage, as opposed to some sort of rebellious rock 'n' roll statement.[7]

Another career opportunity presented itself to Freddie Bell and the Bellboys in late 1955. On the strength of their popularity as a touring group, a few television appearances, and the regional success of "Hound Dog," film producer Sam Katzman cast the band in a motion picture. At the time, "Rock Around the Clock" by Bill Haley and His Comets was one of the most popular rock 'n' roll songs in the country. Hoping to capitalize on the song's popularity and gain a foothold in the teenage movie market, Columbia Pictures charged Katzman with producing a film for young people with the same title as Haley's song. The end result was a hastily put together teen film starring Bill Haley and His Comets, the Platters, Tony Martinez, popular Cleveland disc jockey Alan Freed, and Freddie Bell and the Bellboys. The simple plot was a fictionalized account of the rise of rock 'n' roll designed to showcase the music. The Bellboys performed two songs in the film, a forgettable tune called "Teach You to Rock" and a snappy dance number called "Giddy-Up-A Ding Dong," both co-written by Bell and his Philadelphia friend Pep Lattanzi. "It took eleven days to make that film," Bell later told an interviewer. "It launched my rock 'n' roll career, which I had never really thought of. I was always a saloon singer." Neither song from the film sold well in the United States, but "Giddy-Up-A Ding Dong" became a hit for the Bellboys in England and Australia.[8]

Despite the exposure from the film, Freddie Bell and the Bellboys were still never first-tier rock 'n' rollers. On the road, they remained a variety act that featured up-tempo music, slick moves, and silly chatter between numbers. Their act was tailor-made for Las Vegas, which is where they settled as they became more popular. "They are a loud, comedy, special material aggregation," one Las Vegas newspaper reported. "Their format is strong in the blues department, laced with comic-like material which is well choreographed. . . . No dish for squares." The group played multiple casinos in the area, but had the greatest success at the Sands, where they set up shop in the casino's Silver Queen Bar and Lounge for engagements that ran weeks at a time. It was there, in the spring of 1956, that Freddie Bell and the Bellboys crossed paths with an up-and-coming rock 'n' roll singer from Memphis, Tennessee, who was making his first professional appearance in the city. While no one knew it at the time, the encounter would alter the course of American music history.[9]

The story of Elvis Presley has been well-chronicled. He was born to Vernon and Gladys Presley in Tupelo, Mississippi, on January 8, 1935. His twin brother, Jesse, died at birth, leaving Elvis to grow up an only child. The Presleys never had much money. Vernon had trouble holding a job, and at one point served some time in prison for his part in a clumsy check-forging scheme with a couple of friends. Long-suffering Gladys worked a variety of jobs to help the family limp along financially, but she was barely able to make ends meet. The family moved to Memphis when Elvis was young, and he was associated with that city for the rest of his life. The Presleys lived in boarding houses and public housing, and as a teenager Elvis worked odd jobs to bolster the family income. He also developed an early interest in a wide range of music, including rhythm and blues, country, and gospel.

In the fall of 1949, Elvis entered the ninth grade at Humes High School in Memphis. He was reserved in his manner, but over time he developed a personality and image that stuck out among his classmates. As he got older, Presley shunned standard blue jeans in favor of black slacks and wore his shirts and jackets with the collars perpetually turned up. He also grew sideburns and, for the period, long hair that he sometimes wore slicked back. Some later described the younger Elvis Presley as shy, but he was bold enough to occasionally bring his guitar to school and perform in front of his classmates. He was a bit of an outcast, and an occasional target for bullies because of his different look, but among some of his peers he was an intriguing figure. Many did not really know what to think of him, and branded him as "peculiar," a term that in the South had limitless connotations. "By tenth and eleventh grade Elvis was bringing his guitar in more and more often to sing at little class events like a homeroom party," Presley's high school friend George Klein later wrote. "By senior year, Elvis was very clearly different. . . . But at the same time, as distinctive as his look was, he was low-key about it and never seemed to be angling for any special attention. He got his notoriety in a quiet but unmistakable way."[10]

Even before stardom hit, Presley had a quiet but powerful charisma that seemed to spring from friction generated through the push and pull of his innate cockiness and an equally pronounced feeling of inferiority. His character was complicated and contradictory. He was naturally reserved, but driven to perform, a reticent young man who desperately wanted attention. "He was just so different," early girlfriend Dixie Locke told author Peter Guralnick many years later. "To watch him you would think, even then, he was really shy. What was so strange was that he would do anything to call attention to himself, but I really think he was doing it to prove something to himself rather than to the people around him. I think he knew that he was different."[11]

As was the case with all southerners of his era, the complicated racial dynamics of the world in which Presley lived also had a great effect on him. Part of his being "different" as a performer as he became famous involved race and racial identity. He was white in a rigidly segregated society, but as a singer he embraced a style and presentation traditionally associated with African American artists, and he did so with ease. He was at his best singing R&B rather than ballads, and like rock 'n' roll itself, his act ultimately had blues as its foundation, but would also be a distillation of other musical forms, including country and gospel. Some of the music that influenced him directly as a youngster came through the Memphis radio airwaves. Presley and many other white teenagers in the city were familiar with WDIA and its all-Black format. They also listened to a wild, white disc jockey named

Dewey Phillips, who sometimes played R&B records on his nighttime program *Red Hot & Blue* on another Memphis station, WHBQ. Along with other like-minded white teenagers, Presley made routine pilgrimages to the East Trigg Avenue Baptist Church, pastored by influential African American minister W. Herbert Brewster. It was a Black church that on Sunday nights set aside special seating for whites who wanted to listen to the congregation's gospel choir. "Elvis Presley had been listening [to Black gospel music] long before he became famous, as a boy living in the public housing projects," Memphian Benjamin Hooks, longtime executive director of the NAACP, later told an interviewer. "I remember Herbert Brewster had a great church, the East Trigg [Avenue] Baptist Church, and in the early fifties Elvis Presley and about a hundred white teenagers would be there every Sunday night. We taught them how to clap, because they clapped off beat, and sang off tune, but they learned it." All these compelling elements of Presley's character and upbringing further evolved over time, but they were already present in May of 1953 as he finished his senior year at Humes High School.[12]

Not long after graduating, Presley worked up the courage to visit the Memphis Recording Service at 706 Union Avenue. Sam Phillips owned the place. For a small fee, amateur singers and musicians could record a song and take the acetate home. The story of Elvis Presley crossing paths with Sam Phillips ultimately gave rise to a creation myth regarding Presley's career. A popular version of how the young singer came to make his first record holds that he nervously entered Sam Phillips's studio to make a recording as a birthday gift for his mother (whose birthday was actually months away). Phillips heard Presley sing, immediately recognized his gifts, and decided to work with him and record him in a commercial context. After trying several songs with a backup band consisting of Scotty Moore on guitar and Bill Black on bass, the makeshift group hit on an old blues remake titled "That's Alright." The record took Memphis by storm and laid the foundation for Presley to soon claim the crown "King of Rock 'n' Roll." Race was also a critical element of the tale. As the story goes, Phillips had been looking for a "white kid" who could sing as well as the African American artists he had been recording. When Elvis walked through the door and started singing, Phillips instinctively knew that he had found his man.

While this version of events has some truth in it, Presley's first encounter with Sun was much more complicated, and much less exciting. He probably was nervous when he walked into Phillips's studio, but he was not just a green kid whose sole purpose was to make a recording for his mother. Presley was interested in performing as a pastime, and maybe even as a permanent job. Where he got the idea to visit Phillips is open to conjecture, but Presley and his friends listened to Black music on WDIA and were familiar with the station's on-air talent, including disc jockeys like Rufus Thomas, who had recorded for Sun. The young singer was interested in R&B music, and it was common knowledge around town that Phillips was as well. Articles about what Phillips was up to also ran in local newspapers. Presley may have simply taken Phillips at his word when he advertised that the Memphis Recording Service would "record anything, anywhere, anytime." Marion Keisker, who was Phillips's key administrative assistant and a radio personality in her own right, was the first person Presley spoke to when he entered the building. According to Keisker, Presley asked if he could make a record, and also asked her if she knew any bands that might need a singer. She then asked him who he sounded like, and Presley's answer would become part of his legend. "I don't sound like nobody," he reportedly said.[13]

Presley recorded two songs at the studio that day in the summer of 1953, a syrupy lover's lament titled "My Happiness" and "That's When Your Heartaches Begin," a song that was a hit for the Ink Spots back in 1941. There are two debated versions of what actually took place at the session: one has Phillips making the recording, while the other has Keisker running the equipment and later playing the recordings for Phillips, who had been out of the office. Regardless of who was actually present, Presley made the acetates, and if Phillips had any type of dramatic reaction to the young singer's first recordings, he did not express it, and it would be months before Phillips recorded Presley in a serious way. After that first primitive session, Presley dropped by the Sun office from time to time, just to check in. He usually spoke with Keisker, who remained aware of him and kept his contact information on file. He recorded two more songs at Sun in January of 1954, "I'll Never Stand in Your Way" and "It Wouldn't Be the Same Without You," both forgettable ballads. Still nothing occurred to suggest that Presley would ever have a career in the entertainment business. Phillips did not dismiss Presley, but he did not immediately embrace him either.

Finally, in late June of 1954, and apparently at the repeated suggestion of Marion Keisker, Phillips called on Presley to come in and record another ballad. The session went nowhere, but Philips's did not give up on the young singer. Not long afterward, he enlisted local guitarist Scotty Moore to talk with Presley. Moore hung around the studio and occasionally served as an unofficial talent scout for Sun. He also had his own group, a country outfit called the Starlite Wranglers that included bassist Bill Black. "Give him a call," Phillips instructed the guitarist. "Ask him to come over to your house and see what you think." On the evening of July 3, 1954, Moore set up a meeting at his house with Presley, and the singer came over with his guitar the next day, dressed for the occasion in a lacy white shirt, pink pants with a black stripe down the legs, and white buck shoes. Bill Black came over later and the three men talked music and jammed. One thing that struck Moore as unusual was the sheer number and types of songs that the Tupelo, Mississippi, transplant had in his brain. "I guess what impressed me the most was how uncanny it was that Elvis knew so many songs," he later said. "Everything from Eddie Arnold to Billy Ekstine, just about every damn song in the world." After the meeting broke up, Black told Moore that he was not overly impressed, but Moore thought that Presley had a decent voice and good musical timing.[14]

On July 5, 1954, Phillips brought Presley, Moore, and Black into the studio for what would become an historic recording session. Phillips manned the equipment as the three musicians ran through several ballads, none of which seemed to click. Then, during a break, as the session was winding down, Presley freelanced a faster-paced blues tune called "That's Alright," written and first recorded by Arthur "Big Boy" Crudup in the 1940s. It immediately caught Phillips's attention in the control room. "Elvis still had his guitar—his flat top around his neck with the strap on the shoulder," Phillips later told an interviewer, "and he cut down on 'That's Alright.'" As Presley flailed away on his guitar and sang, Moore and Black rallied to accompany him. "At the time, Bill was on his bass," Moore recalled. "When Elvis started singing, [Bill] leaped up and began playing. Then I joined in." Suddenly, the atmosphere in the room brightened, and Phillips suggested that they record a few takes. "Man, the minute I heard that," he remembered, "I said 'Lord, if we can just attach a few little appendages to this thing, it's going to make some noise that satisfies the soul.'"[15]

Blown away by what he had just heard, Phillips later took the acetate to his friend Dewey Phillips (no relation), a popular disc jockey at WHBQ. Dewey Phillips was a true renegade, and something of an eccentric, to put it mildly. Beloved by whites and African Americans alike, especially teenagers, he had a rapid-fire, hillbilly radio delivery that amused and amazed his listeners. His nightly *Red Hot & Blue* show ran from 9:00 p.m. to midnight and featured a random but raucous mix of many different styles of music. Jerry Schilling, a Presley confidant during the singer's peak years, later describe Phillips as "a half-crazed, speed-talking wild man of a disc jockey" who played "an inspired mix of R&B records, country boogie, hard-core blues, pure gospel, and a few love songs from the silkiest harmony groups." Many years later, Scotty Moore called the radio man, who was also a master of the double-entendre, "a moon-faced country boy" who "taunted his listeners with nonsensical exuberance and language that did not endear him to the parents of teenagers."[16]

Phillips was willing to play songs by newcomers on his show. He loved Presley's version of "That's Alright," and played it on his program not long after Sam brought it to him. The record was an instant hit, and telephone calls and telegrams poured into WHBQ requesting the song and asking about Presley. Dewey interviewed the singer on his show, pointing out to his audience that Presley had attended Humes High School, which also let them know that he was white. Suddenly, and without warning, Sun had thousands of back orders for "That's Alright," and Sam hustled to produce a B-side so that the record could be sold. This turned out to be a rockabilly version of the Bill Monroe bluegrass classic "Blue Moon of Kentucky," which also caught on with listeners. According to newspaper sources, the record sold over six thousand copies in the Memphis area in the three weeks after its release. Overnight, Presley became a celebrity in the city, and he started playing "That's Alright" and "Blue Moon of Kentucky" at public appearances, backed by Moore and Black. He also began developing a stage persona that was controversial for the era. As he played his guitar and sang on stage, his body twitched a little, and he bounced up and down to the rhythm of whatever he was singing. According to Scotty Moore, who watched the Presley phenomenon unfold, girls in the audience went wild when Elvis started to gyrate, but it took a while for the singer and the rest of the band to figure out what was going on. "He stood on the balls of his feet," Moore recalled, "and in playing his guitar and singing he would get to kind of bouncing. Well, when he started bouncing, his britches leg started shaking, and the girls out in the first two or three rows started screaming and hollering, and nobody knew really what it was all about. . . . Of course, after we found out, we started embellishing and embellishing, and didn't we embellish."[17]

A whirlwind of activity followed, as both "That's Alright" and "Blue Moon of Kentucky" got more regional attention. By August 1954, *Billboard* had become aware of Presley, calling him a "strong new talent" and giving the record a positive review. "Presley is a potent new chanter who can sock over a tune in either the country or the R&B markets," the notice read. "On this new disc he comes through with a solid performance of an R&B-type tune, and then on the flip side does another fine job with a country ditty." A star in Memphis, Presley played regular dates at dance clubs and beer joints, and signed a contract with Sun to make more records. "That's Alright" was a favorite on jukeboxes, and "Blue Moon of Kentucky" made the regional country and western charts. This was enough to get the young singer a tryout on the *Grand Ole Opry* in Nashville. Presley did not fit in with the more conservative country crowd at the *Opry,* who offered polite but less than enthusiastic applause after his performance there on October 5, 1954. Undeterred by the experience, Presley not long afterward won a spot on the *Louisiana Hayride,* a popular Shreveport, Louisiana-based radio program that was a bit like the *Opry* but more open to offering fresh talent an opportunity.[18]

It did not take long for Presley to establish himself on the *Hayride.* "Elvis Presley, Memphis' swift-rising hillbilly singing star, is now a regular on the Louisiana Hayride Show," the *Commercial Appeal* reported in Memphis on October 20, 1954. "The Hayride specializes in picking promising young rural rhythm talent, and it took just one guest appearance last Saturday for the young Memphian to become a regular."[19] The *Hayride* offered Presley both exposure and the opportunity to mingle with other popular stars. He performed on the show every Saturday night and toured the South backed by Moore, Black, and Shreveport native D. J. Fontana, a new addition to the band, on drums. He periodically returned to Memphis to record more songs for Sam Phillips that were destined to become rockabilly classics. These included covers of blues and R&B tunes, "Good Rockin' Tonight," "Milkcow Blues Boogie," "Baby, Let's Play House," and "Mystery Train." Despite an obvious penchant for blues-based material, some promoters billed Presley as a country act, likely in an effort to increase tickets sales in the white community, and in a deeper sense because they could not process the concept of a white performer so successfully blurring the lines between white and Black music. Presley's public appearances became more chaotic as he became better known. At his shows, girls screamed louder and crowds became less and less restrained.

Presley's star continued to rise in 1955, but not without significant changes to the business end of his career. Scotty Moore had originally served as Presley's manager when he and the band were just starting out, but as things became more complicated, Bob Neal took over. Neal was a well-connected Memphis radio personality. He was friendly with Sam Phillips and was able to organize better bookings for the singer. "[Elvis] was greatly anxious for success," Neal later reflected. "From the very first he had ambition to be nothing in the ordinary, but to go all the way. He was impatient. He would say 'We got to figure out how to do this. We got to get ahead.'" Neal provided Presley's career with much needed structure, but his tenure as manager was short-lived. Within a year he gave up the position to the man who would dominate Presley's career for the rest of his life, a former carney with a shadowy past who used the alias "Colonel" Tom Parker.[20]

One of the most controversial figures in entertainment history, Tom Parker's personal origins were a bit murky. Credible sources state that he was born in the Netherlands as Andreas Cornelis van Kuijk on June 26, 1909, and came to America illegally as a teenager. He changed his name and later told people that he had been born and orphaned in West Virginia. A schemer even as a young man, Parker began his career touring the United States as a carnival worker and eventually settled in the Tampa, Florida, area, where many of the shows spent the winter months. Through luck, sheer determination, or perhaps just an instinctive ability to pull off the long con, he gravitated toward music management, establishing ties in Nashville's music circles by promoting country acts around Tampa. He managed singer Eddy Arnold for several years during the late 1940s and early 1950s, overseeing Arnold's rise to prominence. From there, he went on to manage Hank Snow, and with Snow formed an entertainment management business. Along the way, Parker received the honorary title "Colonel" in Louisiana's state militia through an old acquaintance who had somehow become an aid to the state's governor, Jimmy Davis. While it was strictly an unearned, honorary title, many people would refer to Parker simply as "The Colonel" throughout his entire show business career.[21]

Exactly when Parker first became aware of Presley is hard to pin down, but once he noticed the singer, he was relentless in his pursuit. Parker began showing up at Presley shows and ingratiating himself with the singer and his family. Knowing that Parker had national connections through his relationships with Arnold and Snow, Neal sought Parker's help with bookings, a move that ended up being the beginning of the end of Neal's tenure as Presley's manager. A master manipulator, Parker signed on as a "special advisor" to Presley, and later, once Neal's original management contract expired, became the singer's official full-time manager. From that point forward, Parker had singular control of Presley's career.[22]

With Parker at the helm, Presley would become the most popular rock 'n' roll singer in the world, but his unparalleled success came at a price. Through the years, Parker kept an unusually high percentage of Presley's earnings for himself, and many of his management decisions came under scrutiny. Many believed—and there was certainly ample evidence to suggest—that he lacked any sort of moral compass, and saw Presley only as a meal ticket. "There was something about his demeanor that bothered me," Scotty Moore said many years later when describing his first meeting with the Colonel. "The more Parker talked, the less I trusted him. On paper, he seemed just what we needed to get over the hump. He had what we needed most: connections. . . . I didn't know him well enough to dislike him. My reaction to him was purely instinctive." Horace Logan, the producer of *Louisiana Hayride,* was more blunt when he stated, "He called himself 'Colonel' Tom Parker—although he was no more of a real colonel than I am. And he came with just one purpose in mind: to take total control of Elvis Presley and claim half of every dollar the kid would ever make."[23]

Regardless of what anyone thought about him, no one could deny that Parker worked hard to promote his client. He secured more and better bookings for the rising star, and negotiated a recording contract with a major label. In November of 1955, RCA Victor purchased Presley's rights from Sun for a reported $35,000, plus $5,000 for Presley for unpaid royalties. The sale would be questioned and written about extensively for decades, but at the time the price represented a great deal of money for Phillips, who was strapped for cash. It was a price that Phillips set, and a price that he never thought RCA Victor would pay. "I made a damn proposition I didn't think they'd take," he said. "I didn't think they'd be fool enough to take it. And it was the eleventh hour before they did take it." The money allowed him to expand his operation and better market some of his other artists. "People have asked me repeatedly, 'do you regret selling Elvis Presley,'" he told one interviewer many years later. "I do not, and I did not, and I will not." Ironically, one reason that Phillips found himself with cash flow problems was the legal entanglements he had been involved in over copyright issues. This included his battle with Don Robey over "Hound Dog," a song that was later a huge hit for Presley.[24]

In January 1956, Presley recorded "Heartbreak Hotel," his first big record for RCA Victor and the song that established him as a national star. By the middle of the year it was at the top of both the *Billboard* country and pop charts, a staggering accomplishment. He and his band continued touring, and Parker negotiated the singer's first national television appearances, a string of spots on the CBS variety program *Stage Show.* Jackie Gleason produced the show, which was hosted by big band leaders (and brothers) Tommy and Jimmy Dorsey. In the years to come, Gleason would always be quick to remind anyone interested that it was he—not Ed Sullivan—who gave the singer his first major television exposure. Presley appeared on the show six times during the first three months of 1956, and his popularity grew with each appearance. "He is some showman," entertainment journalist Earl Wilson wrote in his nationally syndicated column after one show. "He writhes and contorts and suffers through a song, and the kids love it." Interviewed later about his increasingly animated appearances, Presley said, "I didn't copy my style from anybody. . . . I jumped around 'cause it's the way I feel. My stuff's got a beat and I just can't listen to it and stand still." Film producer Hal Wallis saw at least one of the shows and was impressed to the point that he began negotiations for a movie contract with the singer.[25]

On April 3, 1956, Presley moved up the television food chain with a performance on the *Milton Berle Show.* The variety program was a step up from the Dorseys' *Stage Show* because Berle was an established television personality. Nicknamed "Mr. Television," he was the medium's first big star, enjoying great success beginning in the late 1940s. Like other older performers, Berle did not know what to think of the rising young star, and was reluctant to book him, but the potential to bolster his show's recently sagging ratings won out. The week of Presley's appearance, the show was a special broadcast from San Diego in front of an audience of mostly sailors and their dates on the deck of the USS *Hancock.* The actress Esther Williams and the Harry James Band with drummer Buddy Rich were also on the program. Always the comedian, Berle dressed in a gaudy, over-braided admiral's uniform to introduce Presley, telling the crowd, "This is the first time the *Hancock* is going to rock and roll while still anchored." Presley received an enthusiastic welcome and sang "Heartbreak Hotel," along with another recently released hit, "Blue Suede Shoes." Millions tuned in, and within a few weeks Berle booked the singer for a return appearance.[26]

Because of the show's setting and the nature of the military crowd, the positive response from the audience did not reach the unbridled mayhem that Presley was getting used to on the road. The same could not be said of a concert he gave the next night to a civilian crowd of around 11,000—mostly female—at a local arena in San Diego. Presley performed eight songs, creating such a frenzy that promoters had to call in the police. "Presley emitted a wave of almost hypnotic power over his young fans, many of whom squealed, clapped and even stomped their delight," reporter Barbara Schlecht wrote of the spectacle. "We had the feeling that the building would almost disintegrate when the rubber-legged singer reached the highest point in his performance." In a similar vein, an Associated Press account stated, "Presley sings with sensual movements not unlike those of a burlesque queen. The effect on the bobby soxers was such that the arena manager had to call out the police and a platoon of shore patrol to help quell the mob that pursued Presley to a barricaded dressing room."[27]

Immediately after the shows in San Diego, Presley embarked on another

Milton Berle (*left*) and Elvis Presley (*right*), photographed during Presley's controversial second appearance on Berle's television program.
Charlie Gillett Collection/Getty Images.

tour, and after some wrangling by Tom Parker he began a two-week engagement at the New Frontier Hotel in Las Vegas. These shows ended up being an anomaly as far as Presley's tours were concerned. Touted as an "extra added attraction" on a bill that featured the Freddy Martin Orchestra and comedian Shecky Greene, the singer was out of place in front of a mostly middle-aged crowd. He stumbled through his set, with some patrons leaving and others offering only mild, polite applause at the end of each number. "They weren't my kind of audience," Presley later told a reporter. "It was strictly an adult audience. The first night I was absolutely scared stiff." Drummer D. J. Fontana later remembered, "I don't think the people were ready for Elvis. He was mostly for teenage kids . . . and here we were three little pieces making all that noise, and they [the audience] were eating $50 and $60 steaks." The critics were also less than thrilled with the performances. *Newsweek* compared Presley's act to "a jug of corn liquor at a champagne party," while local reviewer Bill Willard wrote in the *Las Vegas Sun,* "For teenagers, the long, tall Memphis lad is a whiz; for the average Vegas spender and showgoer, a bore. His musical sound with his combo is uncouth, matching to a great extent the lyric content of his nonsensical songs."[28]

While the Vegas appearances were far from stellar, Presley's stay in the city was not a total disaster. Parker scheduled a matinee performance for a boisterous crowd of teenagers on the Saturday after they all arrived that was more in line with the singer's usual shows. While he was in town, Presley also got to rub elbows with other celebrities, including Liberace, who was one of his mother's favorite performers. Photographers snapped a few pictures of the two men together, and Presley got the flamboyant pianist's autograph. The singer also seemed to fall in love with the city. During his off hours he made the rounds, took in as many shows as possible, and in general enjoyed the nightlife. "Man, I really like Vegas," he later told an interviewer. "I'm going back there the first chance I get." From that point forward, he visited the city frequently, before famously conquering it as a performer a little over a decade later.[29]

One act that Presley took in during that first trip to the city was Freddie Bell and the Bellboys, and his interest in the group ultimately made the entire visit to Las Vegas worthwhile. Fresh off their appearance in *Rock Around the Clock,* Bell and his band had a popular show at the Silver Queen Lounge in the Sands Hotel. How Presley first became aware of them is up for conjecture. He may have just stumbled on their act as he caroused during his off hours, or he could have been drawn to the group because of publicity lauding their movie appearance. Entertainment columnist Forrest Duke later claimed that he had introduced Presley and Bell one night as he was giving Presley a tour of the Vegas lounges. Regardless of how they first crossed paths, Presley seemed to take a shine to Bell, and visited the Silver Queen Lounge several times with his own band to take in Bell's show.[30]

The future "King of Rock 'n' Roll" was particularly enamored with the Bellboys' performance of "Hound Dog," which they did as a choreographed comedy number far removed from Big Mama Thornton's original version. Scotty Moore later said that Presley knew about Thornton's recording, but was immediately drawn to Bell's treatment as something that he might be able to use in his own stage show. "When we heard them perform that night, we thought the song would be a good one for us to do as comic relief when we were on stage," Moore later wrote in his autobiography. "We loved the way they did it. They had a piano player who stood up and played—and the way he did his legs, they looked like rubber bands bending back and forth." Presley was also comfortable with Bell's lyrics, which were significantly different from the original. If he was aware of Thornton's record, he was also aware that it represented a woman singing to a man, which he obviously could not pull off. "Jerry Leiber and Mike Stoller wrote the song for Big Mama Thornton, but Freddie Bell and the Bellboys had a different set of lyrics," Moore said. "Elvis got the lyrics from those guys. He knew the original lyrics but didn't use them."[31]

It did not take long for Presley to zero in on "Hound Dog." "Elvis would come in every night to see me at the Sands," Bell later remembered. "He was at the Frontier on a bill with Shecky Greene and Freddy Martin. He said 'I love that song,' so I gave him my recording." Bell seemed eager for Presley to record the number, probably hoping that it would give the Bellboys some publicity. Apparently, there was also some talk that Freddie Bell and the Bellboys might open for Presley on tour, but that never happened. Presley took Bell's recording and learned it word for word, and he and the band started practicing "Hound Dog" using Bell's arrangement. "We took that [arrangement] from a band we saw in Vegas, Freddie Bell and the Bellboys," drummer D. J. Fontana later said. "They were doing the song kinda like that. We went out there every night to watch them. [Elvis] would say: 'let's go watch that band. It's a good band!' That's where he heard Hound Dog, and shortly thereafter he said: 'Let's try that song.'" According to some sources, Presley and his band performed "Hound Dog" for the first time on stage on May 15, 1956, to close a show at Ellis Auditorium in Memphis.[32]

While Presley copied Bell's version of "Hound Dog" on stage, the singer was more than likely familiar with Big Mama Thornton's original version. Jerry Leiber and Scotty Moore later mentioned that Elvis knew the original, and it would have been almost impossible for him not to have been familiar with it, considering his background and musical tastes. Presley was a fan of blues and R&B music. He listened to it on Memphis radio stations, and he was familiar with the songs and artists involved. "Hound Dog" was not an obscure song in the R&B world, having been a big hit for Thornton, so anyone interested in R&B music of the period would have known it, and would have probably heard it multiple times on their favorite R&B radio station. Presley was also very familiar with Beale Street in Memphis, which meant he knew about Rufus Thomas, who had recorded "Bear Cat," the infamous "Hound Dog" answer song, for Sam Phillips.

Regardless of whether it was Thornton's offering or Bell's reworked version, Presley's embrace of "Hound Dog" complicated a narrative that would later develop around the song. Many would come to believe that the song's story was a simple tale of Presley hearing Thornton's original version and copying it, adding to the long list of white artists of the rock 'n' roll era who profited from music originally recorded by African Americans. One interpretation—promoted by Thornton herself—held that Presley somehow stole the song and made an obscene amount of money from it at Thornton's expense. This is an easily believable scenario considering that the entire chain of events took place in the 1950s Jim Crow South. Presley's first hit had been "That's Alright," a song written and recorded by an African American bluesman whose original version was lost in the fray as the Presley phenomenon blossomed. Add to all this the fact that there was a period of time—roughly between 1958, when Presley entered the US Army, and 1964, when the Beatles came to America—when record companies regularly produced watered down versions of music by Black artists to sell to white teenagers. The most glaring example of this exercise was probably Pat Boone's 1962 version of the Little Richard hit "Tutti Frutti."[33]

One could argue that putting Presley and someone like Pat Boone in the same category, using "Hound Dog" as an example, does Presley a disservice.

The story of the song is not that cut and dry. "Hound Dog" did not originate in the African American community. It was written by two white teenagers who had talked themselves into believing that they could relate to African American culture at the most basic level. Willie Mae Thornton's delivery and her explosive interpretation made her version of the song an R&B hit, but Presley's version was not a direct copy of Thornton's record. It was a copy of Bell's record, complete with altered tempo and lyrics. "He got the song from Freddie Bell and the Bellboys," Leiber later said. "He did not learn the song from Mama's record." Presley performed the song in a different key, and initially as more of a novelty number, just like the Bellboys. As for Presley "stealing" his first hit, "That's Alright," from Arthur Crudup, Presley's initial brush with the song at Sun was an accident. One could argue that the first time he, Scotty Moore, and Bill Black played that song in the studio, it was more of an impromptu homage than something they thought they could record. It was apparently Sam Phillips who thought the song might have value, though there was no guarantee at the time that it would sell.

Throughout his life, Presley was also quick to acknowledge the African American influence in his early music. "A lot of people think I started this business," he told *Jet* magazine in 1957, "but rock 'n' roll was here long before I came along. Nobody can sing that kind of music like colored people. Let's face it: I can't sing it like Fats Domino can. I know that. But I always liked that kind of music." Both Nat D. Williams and Rufus Thomas, local Memphis music heroes, maintained that when Presley was starting out, he had a significant following in the city's African American community. The singer's African American contemporaries at the national and international levels, including Little Richard and James Brown, often spoke fondly of Presley and did not seem to hold grudges against him in terms of cultural appropriation.[34]

While the exploitation of African American recording artists was a common practice dating back to the dawn of recorded sound, casting Presley as one of the primary villains of the cause during the 1950s might be a bit harsh. As for "Hound Dog," the song's creation and ultimate introduction into American popular culture was too convoluted to view singularly in racial terms, even though the Presley phenomenon would generate many race-based discussions in the years to come. Johnny Otis, who had his own entanglements with "Hound Dog," later cut to the chase when asked in an interview about the singer. "[Presley was] a fine creative artist and a revolutionary figure in American Music," Otis said, "but the kings of rock 'n' roll were Fats Domino, Little Richard, Chuck Berry and B. B. King. . . . He's a fine creative artist and he's got a lot of originality, too. But were he not white, brother, he wouldn't have made it the way that he did." Based on some of his own statements, Presley might have agreed with that assessment himself.[35]

For Presley, "Hound Dog" was an instant hit with live audiences, and he started using the number to close his shows. His dynamic, sexually suggestive presentation transformed the song from a Las Vegas novelty number into something much more raw and dangerous, and it became one of his signature tunes. "The crowd was so loud his voice could hardly be heard," one reviewer wrote after a show on May 22, 1956, in Des Moines, Iowa. "Every move brought more screams. For his last number, he sang 'Hound Dog' while he wrestled the microphone to the floor of the stage. As he knelt near the edge of the stage, many teenagers stretched out their hands to touch him." The song caused a great stir with live audiences, but that was nothing compared to the controversy generated when Presley introduced "Hound Dog" to millions of Americans during his second appearance on the *Milton Berle Show.* By that time, some in the press were already referring to the singer as "perhaps the most controversial figure in the history of recorded music."[36]

Presley's second appearance on Berle's television program was legendary. It was the show's season finale, and the other guests included actress Deborah Paget, comic actor Arnold Stang, television personality Irish McCalla, and the Les Baxter Orchestra. On June 2, 1956, three days before the program, Presley boarded a plane in Memphis and flew out to the West Coast for two performances in Oakland, California. At both shows he faced a mob of barely controllable teenage girls who "expressed their delight by swaying to the rhythm, tapping their feet, pulling their hair, weeping, writhing in the aisles, and shrieking their delight." In addition to the band, the act now included the Jordanaires, a gospel quartet who served as backup singers during some numbers. Music writer Ralph J. Gleason was at one of the appearances, which he later described as "the first show I'd seen that had the true element of sexual hysteria in it. There'd been appearances by all kinds of other music stars, back to Fats Domino and Chuck Berry and including the Everly brothers and Paul Anka, but never anything like what Elvis produced." An extra police contingent had to protect Presley from being overwhelmed by the crowd as he left the stage. A somewhat shell-shocked Gordon Stoker, one of the Jordanaires, later told a reporter, "I've never seen anything to compare to this guy. The reaction he gets is the wildest I've ever seen."[37]

After the Oakland shows, Presley traveled to Los Angeles, where he and his entourage checked into the Hollywood Knickerbocker Hotel on Ivar Avenue. They went to the NBC-TV studios in Burbank for a few hours of rehearsals on June 4, and the next day returned for the live broadcast. Some later said that while Berle was friendly, he seemed slightly nervous or ill at ease about Presley's appearance. At the time, the host was under a great deal of pressure. While he was still a popular media figure, and viewed as one of the founding fathers of television entertainment, he was still a slave to the ratings. His show had begun to slip, playing second fiddle on Tuesday nights to the *Phil Silvers Show* on CBS. Rumor had it that Berle's season finale might mark the end of his show's run. The comedian might have been nervous about Presley because the singer had grown immensely more popular since his first appearance on the show, and for younger viewers at least, he was a bigger star than Berle. Berle now needed Presley for ratings more than Presley needed Berle to advance his career. On top of that, a certain danger and unpredictability accompanied Presley's performances, which was enough to fray the nerves of any host. "This was the last show of the season and [Berle] knew that having Elvis on would kick his ratings way up. I'm sure that's why he was nervous," one observer later said. "But Elvis, as always, was very courteous to him and, believe it or not, spent a lot of the rehearsal time trying to make Milton feel comfortable."[38]

Regardless of what Berle felt at the time, his hour-long program featuring Elvis Presley began at 8:00 p.m. (EST) on Tuesday, June 5, 1956. Berle opened with some jokes, and then some comedy routines before the show went into a commercial break. After the break, Berle introduced Presley, calling him "the new singing sensation all over the country!" The singer was dressed to kill in a light-colored sports jacket, two-tone shirt, wavy black slacks, and highly polished black shoes. He did not wear his own guitar, but had his usual band of Scotty Moore, Bill Black, and D. J. Fontana backing him up. Berle later claimed that it was his idea for Presley to go on stage without the instrument, telling the singer "let 'em see you, son." The band quickly launched into "Hound Dog," a song they had performed many times on stage but would not record for at least another month. It started as the Freddie Bell version, complete with the words "hound dog" repeated at the end of the opening line, but Presley made the song his own through what could only be described as a seismic presentation. As he had been doing at the live shows, D. J. Fontana added a "machine gun" drum flourish at the end of each verse that allowed Presley to accentuate his frantic movements—or "gyrations," as almost every newspaper in the country called them. It was a key addition that made the number much less Vegas and much more rock 'n' roll, and it would become one of the most famous pieces of rock drumming ever. "There was no reason for it," Fontana later said with typical modesty. "I decided to put it in there. [Elvis] said 'Hey, that sounds great, do it every time.'"[39]

It was the end of the performance that created the greatest stir. As they were winding down, the band, at Presley's direction, abruptly slowed the tempo of the song to give it a more bluesy feel that was straight out of a strip joint. It was something that they had done in the past to one degree or another during live performances of the song, a theatrical device that was sexy but also a little bit silly, almost as if it were an inside joke between Presley and the band. The slower tempo also magnified the sexual nature of Presley's stage contortions. That said, it was not something that the band expected him to do on national television. "All of a sudden [Elvis] decided he was going to go into this blues thing," D. J. Fontana later remembered about the performance. "We all looked at each other and said 'what do we do now?' I went back into my roots of playing strip music. I worked in burlesque houses when I was a youngster. . . . It was every man for himself." The spectacle was a highly unusual change of pace for a Tuesday night, prime time television broadcast of the 1950s. As the show went on, the camera made a quick cut to the teenage girls in the audience, many of whom sat transfixed, slowly moving and nodding to the rhythm. "He shakes and wiggles and jumps and bumps," one reporter later wrote. "Its like watching a strip-teaser and a malted milk machine all at the same time." RCA Victor publicist Ann Fulchino had a similar take, later telling a reporter, "Elvis is the equivalent of a male strip teaser, with the exception that he doesn't take his clothes off."[40]

When the band finally finished, the crowd let out a great cheer, and Berle reappeared on stage. "How about my boy," he shouted gleefully, as if he could already feel the boost in his program's ratings. In an attempt at humor, he began jumping around, imitating Presley, before making a few good-natured jokes about the singer's popularity. Presley appeared later in the show—this time with the Jordanaires providing backing vocals—singing a slower song, "I Want You, I Need You, I Love You." As his follow up to "Heartbreak Hotel," it was quickly rising up the charts as well. Just before the show ended, Berle presented Presley with an award from *Billboard* magazine and lauded him as "the fastest rising young singer in the entertainment industry today." Even though Berle still did not quite understand rock 'n' roll, it was obvious that he viewed Presley's appearance as a success.[41]

Elvis Presley's loose, sexually charged performance of "Hound Dog" on the Milton Berle program created a firestorm of protests and pans in the mainstream media. The day after the broadcast, *New York Times* music critic Jack Gould disparaged the singer as a "virtuoso of hootchy kootchy," with "no discernible singing ability." Two days later, *New York Daily News* television critic Ben Gross was even more direct in describing the "grunt and groin antics" of the singer. "Elvis, who rotates his pelvis, was appalling musically," Gross stated. "He gave an exhibition that was suggestive and vulgar, tinged with the kind of animalism that should be confined to dives and bordellos." Others referred to "the Elvis Presley menace" and condemned Presley for "asserting his own primitive masculinity in an unending series of bumps and grinds." To California critic Bob Foster, Presley's "indecent" presentation of "Hound Dog" qualified as "one of the most disgusting and unnecessary performances we have seen on television in a good long time." Berle himself caught a good bit of shrapnel from the criticism, with some media outlets calling Presley's appearance "'Berlesque' at its worst," and complaining "it was bad enough that Berle even had the young man on his show, but why did he keep constantly complimenting him?" Unfazed by the criticism, Berle took it as a good sign for Presley. As a television veteran, the comedian knew that the controversy generated by Presley's appearance represented millions in free publicity for the singer. After receiving piles of protest letters, Berle called Tom Parker and assured him that he had a bona fide star on his hands. A reported 40 million viewers had tuned in.[42]

The appearance was one of the watershed events of Presley's career. Berle was right in that the controversy dramatically increased the singer's already significant public profile. Presley was very popular among teenagers, but afterward he was entrenched in the American consciousness. The controversy also helped rally his young fans behind him, and confirmed what many in Hollywood knew. Elvis Presley had the potential to be a very bankable film star. The singer's career would have likely continued its upward trajectory had he not performed the "Hound Dog" bump and grind on Berle's program, but there is no doubt that the appearance was an accelerant. It also helped popularize the nickname "Elvis the Pelvis," much to Presley's chagrin. As for Presley's personal take on all the hoopla, he consistently claimed that he was doing nothing wrong, and seemed outwardly perplexed that some deemed his music sinful. "My pelvis has nothing to do with what I do," a slightly annoyed Presley told a correspondent from *TV Guide*. "I just get kinda in rhythm with the music. I jump around to it because I enjoy what I'm doing. I'm not trying to be vulgar. I'm not trying to sell any sex. I'm not trying to look vulgar and nasty. I just enjoy what I'm doing and trying to make the best of it."[43]

Presley's appearance on the Milton Berle program led to another major "Hound Dog" incident destined to become part of American popular music lore. This one involved television host Steve Allen. A multi-talented, quick-witted comedian not averse to social comment, Allen started on television in the late 1940s and served as the first host of *The Tonight Show* on NBC. The network gave him his own Sunday night variety program in 1956 in hopes of competing with the formidable *Ed Sullivan Show*, a variety offering on CBS that was a ratings juggernaut. Allen's first broadcast was June 24, 1956, and while he drew a significant audience, he did not come close to beating Sullivan. However, his second broadcast on July 1 would win its 8:00 p.m. (EST) time slot, with Elvis Presley serving as the catalyst for Allen's ratings increase.[44]

Presley's appearance on Allen's program was controversial on a couple of levels. The singer had been booked well in advance, but after his "Hound Dog" performance on Berle's show there was substantial pressure on NBC to cancel the appearance. "NBC brass were appalled at the Elvis Presley torso tossing on Berle's show," one report stated, "and declare they'll have no more of it on their network." Allen also said that he had been "flooded with letters from people in all walks of life" who wanted him to ditch the singer. Prominent columnist Charles Mercer, in a long and detailed treatise that appeared in newspapers all over the country a few days before the broadcast, chastised Allen for keeping the singer on the bill. He stated that Presley lacked talent and appealed only to "a very small but very noisy minority of the immature who have been infected in recent years by the digga-boom convulsions known as rock 'n' roll." In the racist conclusion to his missive, Mercer suggested that if Allen wanted to have a true rock 'n' roller on his show, he should bring one in from Africa. "Any one of those singers and shufflers would be happy to fly over and appear on your show," the columnist wrote. "And you won't have to give him a big car. He'll settle for a bicycle."[45]

Despite all the criticism and network posturing, both Allen and the NBC executives knew that a Presley appearance would deliver ratings, which was the true litmus test for any television performer. Like many of his contemporaries, Allen did not care for rock 'n' roll, and failed to recognize it as an art form, but that did not matter. There was a concrete bottom line involved. Presley meant big viewing numbers, and no network would pass that up. NBC had specifically hired Allen to dethrone Ed Sullivan as the "King of Sunday Nights," and Presley's booking prior to the Berle show was not an accident. The singer was controversial and a potential ratings grabber before that appearance, and his bump and grind "Hound Dog" performance made him an even hotter entertainment commodity. No network could pass that up, no matter how many angry parents, little old ladies, or irritated columnists complained.

NBC announced that it would not cancel Presley, but Allen still had to navigate the controversy. In public statements, he barely disguised his disdain for rock 'n' roll as he defended having Presley on his show. He stated that he would "make sure that [Presley] conducts himself as a gentleman," and he criticized the singer for "thoughtlessly indulging in certain dance movements on his last TV appearance." As for the claim by many that Presley was not a legitimate performer, the host was noncommittal but a little condescending, stating that while millions thought he was talentless, "I am sure additional millions will rise in his defense and say that he has oodles of talent." Allen also made one claim that was blatantly false when referring to

Presley's recent antics. "He knows he made a mistake with the Milton Berle business," Allen said. "And I think he is smart enough not to do it again." Nothing could have been further from the truth. Throughout his life, Presley defended his performance on Berle's show and never gave any indication that he believed he had done anything wrong. It was also of note that Allen made the statement having never talked to Presley about the incident.[46]

Allen hinted at his true feelings about Presley, and rock 'n' roll in general, a couple of weeks before the Presley show aired. In the press, he quoted a letter that he supposedly received from a woman complaining about singer's appearance on the Berle program. "I, too, saw [Presley] and was utterly repelled," the letter read. "Sometimes it seemed to me there's a deliberate plot to degrade the character of Americans. The minds of the people who built this country were not sustained on such fodder." As he referenced the letter and its content, Allen praised its author as "a most intelligent lady." Many years later, with Presley safely dead and therefore unable to defend himself, Allen told a reporter, "Of all the singers who have ever been popular in our culture, he was the most popular. But his songs were the worst, averaged out, that any established singer ever recorded. The fact that someone with so little ability became the most popular singer in history says something significant about our cultural standards." In the end, Allen proved to be just another dusty member of an entertainment generation who was either threatened by or jealous of the rising popularity of rock 'n' roll during the 1950s. He had no problem mocking the phenomenon, yet he also had no problem using it to boost the ratings of his television program.[47]

In the aftermath of Presley's "Hound Dog" performance on the *Milton Berle Show,* one of the practical matters that Allen and his producers had to address was how to make the most of the controversy. A succinct strategy quickly emerged. It involved the claim that they planned to showcase a previously unseen, tamer side of the singer, allowing him to make a "comeback" from the Berle debacle and atone for his past sins. "I naturally had no interest in presenting him vaudeville-style and letting him do his spot as he might in concert," Allen later wrote. In reality, what they meant by "taming" Presley was that they planned to take the raw charisma and intensity that was making him a global superstar and do their best to turn it into one big joke at the singer's expense. They would allow him to sing "Hound Dog," but would make him as uncomfortable as possible by dressing him in white tie and tails, limiting his movements on camera, and forcing him to sing to an actual dog, making the canine the focus of the stage presentation. "Let me assure audiences again," Allen stated three days before the broadcast, "that they will not be offended by Elvis on any program over which I have control. We'll show you a new side of the boy."[48]

Steve Allen's show featuring Elvis Presley aired on Sunday evening, July 1, 1956. Whether or not Allen intentionally tried to humiliate Presley during the appearance has been up for debate for decades. The comedian later called the singer a "solid performer" and claimed that forcing Presley to dress up and sing to a dog was all in the spirit of fun, and that there was no ill will involved. Others viewed the situation differently. For many of those around at the time, as well as for many viewers who were Presley fans, Allen seemed condescending toward the singer when the show aired. Scotty Moore certainly believed it was a hatchet job. "By the time we arrived in New York on July 1 for a performance on television's *Steve Allen Show,* the host was gunning for [Presley]," the guitarist wrote in his memoir. "Elvis gamely went along, giving what certainly had to be one of the most excruciating performances of his career." According to various accounts, Presley later remembered the appearance as "silly" and "embarrassing."[49]

Regardless of what Allen thought of Presley, he knew that the singer's appearance meant big ratings and represented a golden opportunity for the NBC offering to best its rival, the *Ed Sullivan Show,* on CBS. Producers saved Presley's appearance for the second half of the show. Allen introduced him somewhat nervously, making reference to Presley's previous appearance with Berle. The host then assured his audience, "It's our intention to do nothing but a good show. We want to do a show that the whole family can watch and enjoy, and we always do. And tonight we are presenting Elvis Presley in what you might call his first comeback, and at this time it gives me extreme pleasure to introduce the new Elvis Presley." As syrupy orchestral background music played, Presley walked on stage to greet Allen, looking clean and dapper, but much less threatening than usual, in white tie and tails, with white gloves completing the outfit. He carried a top hat that he never put on and quickly discarded. Presley awkwardly removed the gloves as he bantered with Allen, and some in the crowd later said that they thought the singer looked ill at ease. The next day, television critic Mary Cremmen wrote that "Presley's expression which, in the past, alternated between sullen and inscrutable had changed for his new personality from uncomfortable to miserable."[50]

Presley sang two songs that night, backed as usual by Moore, Black, and Fontana, and accompanied by the Jordanaires. The first was "I Want You, I Need You, I Love You," a ballad that showcased the singer's vocal range. It was a slower-paced love song, and as such the accompanying visual of a rock 'n' roll outlaw performing in formalwear was not as stark. As the song ended, Allen reappeared on stage, pushing a small table on which rested a sleepy-eyed basset hound wearing a black bowtie collar and a toy top hat. After mentioning that Presley was actually scheduled to record "Hound Dog" the next day, Allen introduced the song by telling the singer, "I got you a very cute little hound dog right here, and away you go." It was more parody than performance as Presley began singing to the canine. He seemed to recognize the ridiculous nature of what he was doing, and actually laughed a couple of times as he delivered the lyrics, occasionally touching and petting the dog in a good-natured way. When it was all over, he gave a bow and quickly exited stage right. He made one more appearance toward the end of the show, as part of a hokey comedy skit that poked fun at country music, another genre that Allen did not care for. Fellow guests Andy Griffith and Imogene Coca were also in the skit, as was Allen himself.[51]

Generations of Presley fans would cast Allen as a villain for his attempt to "tame" their idol. The host later downplayed the incident, insinuating that Presley himself had willingly altered his style for the program. "We worked [Presley] into the comedy fabric of our program," Allen later wrote. "We certainly didn't inhibit Elvis' then-notorious pelvis gyrations, but I think the fact that he had on formal evening attire made him, purely on his own, slightly alter his presentation."[52] These comments, which came well after the show aired, seem disingenuous in that it was Allen and his producers who had intentionally required Presley to wear the "monkey suit" in the first place. They also intentionally altered the singer's ability to work the room by requiring him to sing not to the live audience, but to a dog functioning as a stationary stage prop. There were also some premeditated production details indicating Allen and his people were worried about the way that Presley might move around. As the singer performed "Hound Dog," the camera angles abruptly changed to hide his lower half during Fontana's machine-gun drum fills and Scotty Moore's guitar solo, the precise moments when Presley had been the most animated on the Berle show.

After the broadcast, Presley went back to his hotel and sat for a chat over a remote feed with syndicated columnist Hy Gardner, who hosted an interview program on NBC's New York affiliate WRCA called *Hy Gardner Calling.* During the course of their conversation, Presley told Gardner that he had fun on the Allen program, but it was obvious that the singer was wrung out from the experience and the controversy surrounding it. He answered Gardner's questions, but did so slouched in a chair, looking tired and distracted, sometimes almost mumbling. He perked up a little when Gardner asked the inevitable questions about his past behavior on stage, be it the Berle show or during his unending string of concert appearances. "I don't feel like I'm doing anything wrong," he told Gardner. "I'm aware of everything I do at all times. . . . I don't see that any type of music would have any bad influence on people when it's only music." When asked if he resented media critics who condemned him, Presley brushed off the question, answering, "Not really. Those people have a job to do, and they do it."[53]

The fallout from the Steve Allen performance was immediate. It pleased many critics that Allen had "cowed" or "dry cleaned" Presley by not allowing him to offend the public with the "horrible howling, yowling, screeching noises" heard on the Berle show. "As you may know by now, I'm not exactly an admirer of the Presley vocal technique," sixty-four-year old Ben Gross wrote. "But millions of youngsters like it and let's hope they enjoyed it. This time, to be truthful, there was nothing to complain about." In his syndicated column, forty-one-year-old Jack O'Brian was more cutting, writing that Allen had forced the singer to follow "the most basic rules of taste and intelligence," and in so doing "proved Presley's excitement is not his voice but his erotic presentation." Presley claimed that he did not read many reviews, and whether that was true or not, he never seemed too rattled by them. In fact, criticism from the older set usually worked in his favor, promoting an "us against them" mentality that made him more attractive to his teenage fans, which in turn sold more records. The more criticism Presley received from their elders, the tighter many 1950s teenagers embraced him. The singer did have at least one defender in the class of major columnists. John Lardner of *Newsweek* actually chastised Allen for trying to "civilize" Presley, writing, "Allen's ethics were questionable from the start. He fouled Presley, a fair-minded judge would say, by dressing him like a corpse in white tie and tails. This is a costume often seen on star performers at funerals, but only when the deceased has specifically requested it in his will. Elvis made no such request—or for that matter, no will. He was framed."[54]

As they processed what they had seen on the *Steve Allen Show*, the emotions of many of the singer's young devotees ranged from disbelief to anger and disgust. For days afterward newspapers all over the country printed letters to the editor from outraged Presley supporters who blamed Allen for abusing their hero. One that appeared in the *Los Angeles Times* was typical. "Gee, it was awful," the fan lamented as she described the show. "They had him tied down in a tuxedo and wouldn't let him move. . . . They've ruined Elvis!" While Presley may not have cared what older folks said about him in the press, he was sensitive to the wants and needs of his young fans. He fed off their energy onstage and knew that they were the foundation upon which his career rested. He did not want to disappoint them, and he especially did not want them to believe that what happened on the *Steve Allen Show* was a sign that he had somehow "sold out" or buckled to societal pressures. Such perceptions could tarnish his image as a rebel, and even threaten his livelihood. "It did worry him," D. J. Fontana later recalled. "He worried about everything. He really did. He always worried about—'well, do you think they liked me?'"[55]

Presley may have been uncomfortable with the performance, but Steve Allen and manager Tom Parker thought that the appearance went well, particularly when the press announced the ratings for the broadcast. If anyone was "cowed" on that fateful Sunday evening, it may have been Ed Sullivan over at CBS. He had countered Allen's show with a tamer offering featuring actors Gregory Peck, Edward G. Robinson, and Lauren Bacall among others paying tribute to the career of film director John Huston. "With the latest teen-age idol in his corner," the *New York Daily News* reported on July 3, "Steve Allen caused the season's upset Sunday night by kayoing Ed Sullivan with a 20.2. Trendex rating to Ed's 14.8. Steve also garnered a 53% share of audience to Sullivan's 39.7%." Translated into layman's language, these numbers represented a huge victory for NBC and the fledgling *Steve Allen Show.* It was also an embarrassing defeat for Sullivan that forced him to reassess and adapt to what was going on in the entertainment marketplace. Regardless of what he wore or who he sang to, Elvis Presley had put the television world on notice that teenage viewers and even curious adults were a force to be reckoned with.[56]

The day after Presley appeared on the *Steve Allen Show,* he and his entourage went to New York's RCA studio for a prearranged recording session, and were met outside by teenage fans carrying signs that read, "We want the gyratin' Elvis" and "We want the real Elvis." Photographer Alfred Wertheimer, who was documenting Presley for RCA, later talked to one of the female fans. "Elvis was too tame," she told him, referring to the Allen appearance. "We want to see Elvis move and we don't care if our parents don't like it. We want the real Elvis. Please tell him what we think, ok?" Presley did not need the photographer's counsel on the matter. He was already well aware of what his young fans thought about the appearance, and it may have been weighing on his mind as the session began. "Hound Dog" was the only song that Presley knew he was in the studio to record that day, though he chose and recorded a couple of others before the session ended. RCA executives were pushing for the song's release after it generated so much controversy on the Berle and Allen programs.[57]

In addition to Presley, the session included his usual band with Moore on guitar, Black on bass, and Fontana on drums, along with the Jordanaires—Gordon Stoker, Hoyt Hawkins, Neal Matthews, and Hugh Jarret—providing backup vocals. Country musician Emidio Vagnoni, known professionally as Shorty Long, came in to play piano. Veteran RCA executive Stephen Sholes was also there as producer, although most accounts say that in the end it was Presley who did most of the producing at the session, especially on "Hound Dog." Alfred Wertheimer, who was also in the room taking photographs, included a detailed account of the session in his 1979 book *Elvis '56: In the Beginning.* "Other artist I had covered were directed by a producer. He was the man in charge," Wertheimer recalled. "With Elvis the mood was casual, relaxed, joking. Steve [Sholes] did not dictate. He managed. And though Elvis was not a forward, take-charge character, he was clearly the one who had to be pleased. When it concerned his music, no one was more serious."[58]

The part of the session that produced "Hound Dog" lasted all morning, and at times was tedious, bordering on torturous. Primitive by later standards, the technical process of making a record in 1956 usually followed a simple pattern. The first step was a few rehearsal takes during which the studio engineer mixed the sound. After that, the singer and the band performed the song from beginning to end as many times as was necessary, with the best take being chosen for the record. The technical constraints of the period did not allow for significant changes or overdubs after the fact. The best performance by the band on a particular day in the studio was the one that the world eventually heard.

Although they were very familiar with "Hound Dog," and had obviously performed it many times, Presley and the band had trouble producing what everyone agreed on as a useable take. Sometimes Presley stumbled over the words, and other times the music was not as crisp as it should have been. "For some reason, we couldn't get the song down on tape the way we performed it live," Scotty Moore later recalled. "We did take after take. Sometimes D. J.'s drums were off beat. Sometimes I was off my solo, my notes wandering off to nowhere." Five takes turned into ten, and ten into fifteen. Around that time, Shorty Long had to leave for another appointment and Gordon Stoker of the Jordanaires replaced him at the piano. As they continued to work, everyone in the room "started glancing at Elvis to check his mood." Presley was frustrated but never lost his temper. Steve Sholes thought take eighteen was a keeper, but the singer was dismissive, claiming that he could do better. In the end, it took thirty-one takes before Presley announced that he was satisfied, much to the relief of all involved. A little later, with less drama, Presley and the band recorded "Don't Be Cruel," penned by master songsmith Otis Blackwell and also destined to become a huge hit, and the ballad "Any Way You Want Me." All in all, it was a full day.[59]

Presley's "Hound Dog" proved to be a strange but provocative hybrid. Rooted in Thornton's tough R&B original, his rendering was more aligned lyrically with the silly version that Freddie Bell and the Bellboys performed onstage, though it was obviously much more powerful. It was an odd but explosive mix of Black and white sensibilities—just like rock 'n' roll itself—with Presley's personal magnetism guaranteeing a hit in the marketplace. Presley brought some of the anger of the original version back into the song through his presentation, delivering an intensity that somehow made Bell's nonsensical lyrics seem perfectly placed. A reviewer for *Billboard* called it "a highly charged rhythm opus in Presley's characteristic style that should enjoy heavy commercial success." Fontana's fiery "rat-a-tat-ratta-tat-tat" drum fills added to the mayhem of the record, as did the blistering guitar work of Scotty Moore. In the end, Elvis Presley's "Hound Dog" was not a perfect song, but it turned out to be a perfect rock 'n' roll anthem.[60]

On July 3, Presley and the band boarded a train for Memphis, where they were on the bill at a charity event the next night. It was a twenty-seven-hour trip that the singer endured, both exhausted from his previous few day's work and elated at the thought of returning home. The July 4 concert took place at Russwood Park, a minor league baseball facility, where fourteen thousand fans saw Presley in top form. Still concerned about the fallout from the *Steve Allen Show,* he took the opportunity to assure the hometown crowd that he was still the same performer they all knew and loved. "You know those people in New York are not going to change me none," he said. "I'm going to show you what the real Elvis is like tonight." Presley closed the show with "Hound Dog" after announcing to the crowd that it would be his next single. As was the case at most of his live appearances, the crowd went wild as the show ended and Presley left the stage. "Dressed in black clothing with a bright red tie," the local newspaper dutifully reported, "[Elvis] whipped himself and the crowd into a frenzy in his last number, 'You Ain't Nothing But a Hound Dog,' before smooth handling by the police wafted him away."[61]

Not long afterward, the fruits of Presley's New York recording session reached the public when RCA Victor released a remarkable record. At the time, when a company released a single disc, it usually designated one side as the "A-side," and the other as the "B-side," with the A-side garnering more attention and being the primary focus of the company's publicity efforts. The B-side was usually a secondary recording that was adequate but not necessarily destined for heavy airplay or sales. On July 21, 1956, RCA Victor released Presley's latest disc, with "Hound Dog" on one side and "Don't Be Cruel" on the other. Both would be massive hits, and it was obvious that neither was a secondary recording. RCA Victor had produced a record that in effect had not one but two A-sides, although "Hound Dog" was originally listed as side B. "It's a swinging disc with two hot sides," a reporter wrote in *Cashbox*. "Definite double-barreled smash." The "Hound Dog"/"Don't Be Cruel" juggernaut was conspicuous in the *Billboard* pop charts for weeks and sold millions of copies. For a while, the songs held the top two spots on the charts, an unusual accomplishment for a single, two-sided record of the period. It also topped the publication's country and R&B charts. Newspapers around the country stated that the record sold 1 million copies in the first two weeks, making it the fastest selling single in history. According to one report, demand was so high that "RCA Victor commandeered every piece of record-making machinery in its factories—and then hired a competitor, Capitol Records, to handle the overflow production."[62]

While "Don't Be Cruel" became a big hit on its own, "Hound Dog" received most of the initial attention when the record came out. The explosive sales figures were a product of Presley's natural career momentum as well as the controversy generated by his appearances with Berle and Allen. "Hound Dog" was also a memorable tune. It was unlike Presley's previous hits in that the title did not give away the subject matter of the recording, and the lyrics did not make complete sense. "Heartbreak Hotel" had obviously been about the heartbreak of a broken relationship, and "I Want You, I Need You, I Love You" was even more obviously a love song. While it was easy to assume that "Hound Dog" had something to do with a relationship, the title did not offer any clues to the song's storyline, and the phrase "you ain't never caught a rabbit" was up for interpretation. While many listeners assumed that it was some kind of southern colloquialism referencing a woman or a relationship, the words actually originated with a Las Vegas lounge singer who was a Pennsylvania native. Most of the teenagers who bought the record were white. They were probably not familiar with Big Mama Thornton's record, or with Freddie Bell, Jerry Leiber, or Mike Stoller. They had no frame of reference for the song's original message. The kids had to figure it all out for themselves, which, coupled with Presley's frantic, fiery delivery, added to the song's overall intrigue. It was also pure rock 'n' roll in that it was a song designed to be felt rather than scrutinized using mainstream or traditional music standards.

Reviews of the new record were somewhat predictable. Many in established press circles continued to despise Presley and all that he stood for, like Red Leiter of the *Indianapolis News,* who accused the singer of performing the song "in grunts and belches." Some established artists who sang in a more traditional manner also disparaged the song, likely because they felt threatened. "When I hear 'Hound Dog,'" crooner Perry Como told a reporter, "I have to vomit a little." Not long after the song's release, even the great Frank Sinatra chimed in. While not mentioning Presley specifically, he called rock 'n' roll "the most brutal, ugly, degenerate, vicious form of expression it has been my displeasure to hear." Many politicians followed suit in an effort to enhance their image as protectors of American morals, a position that might improve their electability. Senator George Smathers of Florida claimed "the airwaves of this country have been flooded with inferior music," while Representative Emanuel Celler of New York complained about "the bad taste that is exemplified by Elvis Presley's 'Hound Dog' music with his animal gyrations."[63]

In the end, the bad press did nothing but enhance Elvis Presley's popularity with the people that counted, his fans. "Hound Dog"—both in attitude and in sales figures—reinforced the fact that rock 'n' roll represented a dramatic change within the entertainment industry, to the discomfort of some in the older generation. It was not a fad, or a flash in the pan, and it represented the rise of a powerful youth culture. While other artists were involved in the process, with each Presley release in 1956 rock 'n' roll further penetrated the American consciousness, and nothing was a bigger release than "Hound Dog." Teenagers could not get enough of it, and parents could not ignore the phenomenon, regardless of how they felt about it. "Presley is here to stay," correspondent Steve Schickel wrote in the *Chicago Tribune* shortly after "Hound Dog" flew up the charts. "Whether the old folks like it or not, the teenagers and their loyalty to what they like will see to that."[64]

Despite the altered lyrics, Presley's "Hound Dog" still credited Leiber and Stoller as the songwriters, with Bell receiving no credit as his changes amounted to "an unauthorized adaptation." Leiber and Stoller would always have a love-hate relationship with Presley's version. They loved the financial rewards and notoriety that it brought them, but were not wild about the song as an artistic statement. They had written it for Big Mama Thornton, and to them Presley's version lacked the spark of the original. The tempo was different and the change in lyrics abandoned the tune's original theme. "I had different feelings," Leiber later said. "The first feeling is the one that washes over any songwriter when he learns he has a hit. He hears the cash register ring. . . . That's a good feeling. But when I heard Elvis's version, I had a bad feeling. I didn't like the way he did it." Stoller expressed similar sentiments. He was annoyed at the alterations, but was more than willing to cash any checks that the song brought him. Both men thought Presley had talent, and they recognized him as a revolutionary figure, but that did not mean that they had to like the way he presented their song.[65]

Leiber actually found out well before Stoller that Presley's version of "Hound Dog" was a hit, which ultimately created an unusual footnote to the song's history. In the spring of 1956, Stoller received a large royalty check for some previous compositions, and he used it to take his wife, Meryl, on a three-month European vacation to "see new sights, hear foreign languages, eat strange foods, sample exotic drinks, and walk down streets where people had walked centuries before." They visited England, Ireland, Belgium, Denmark, and France, and were scheduled to return to the United States in late July. While they were overseas, Presley released "Hound Dog," which quickly rose up the charts. Unaware of the record, Stoller and his wife boarded an ocean liner for the trip home and were soon involved in a dramatic chain of events that almost left Jerry Leiber without a songwriting partner. The liner that they chose for their return trip was the ill-fated *Andrea Doria*.[66]

Bound for New York, the *Andrea Doria* never made it. As it approached the American coast on the night of July 25, 1956, the ship collided with another vessel and began to sink. "The collision was thunderous." Stoller recalled. "Later we learned that we'd been struck in the side by the *Stockholm*, another huge ocean liner. The impact rocked everyone and everything. Immediately our ship started listing to starboard." All hell broke loose as passengers scrambled to save themselves. After much effort, Stoller and his wife made it to a lifeboat, and were later rescued by a passing freighter. Forty-six of the ship's twelve hundred passengers lost their lives in what became one of the twentieth century's most storied maritime disasters. Shaken but unhurt, Stoller made it to New York Harbor, where Jerry Leiber met him at the dock. Leiber threw his arms around Stoller and asked if he was alright, and then blurted out, "We have a hit." He explained that "Hound Dog" was topping the charts, and Stoller at first thought that somehow the Thornton version had been resurrected. Leiber told him no, that it was "some white kid named Elvis Presley" who recorded the song.[67]

One man who took a great interest in the comings and goings of Elvis Presley, and in "Hound Dog" as an entertainment vehicle, was Ed Sullivan. Originally a newspaper columnist, Sullivan for eight years had hosted the most popular variety show on television. He was a steady television presence, and his show was the definition of mainstream. It had a format similar to vaudeville, presenting a wide range of acts on each show, from opera singers and ballet dancers to comedians, jugglers, and animal acts. It had "something for everyone," he boasted. The *Ed Sullivan Show* was also an arbiter of public taste that broadcast nothing too outlandish. It was safe, and the perfect vehicle for entertainers who sought wide exposure. Steve Allen had used Presley to beat Sullivan in the ratings, and for Sullivan this created a quandary. In the past he had been critical of Presley, and of rock 'n' roll in general, but on the other hand he did not like to lose. The singer may have generated controversy, but Sullivan knew a ratings winner when he saw one. Like many of his contemporaries, the fifty-five-year-old host did not fully understand the aesthetic value of what Presley did onstage, but it was obvious that large segments of the viewing public would tune in to watch whatever it was.

After Presley appeared on the *Steve Allen Show*, Sullivan wasted no time contacting Tom Parker about booking the singer. The tremendous ratings that Presley generated gave Parker an advantage in the negotiations. Sullivan needed the singer more than he usually needed other performers, and he wanted to stomp on Allen, who he viewed as a threat. The result was an agreement for Presley to make three appearances on the program for $50,000 total, which at the time was an extraordinary sum. Allen had only paid Presley $5,500 for one show, and Sullivan usually paid established stars like Bing Crosby and Frank Sinatra around $7,500 per appearance. It was a financial windfall for Presley (and Parker) and a further indication of the singer's expanding power in the entertainment industry.[68]

Presley's first appearance on Sullivan's Sunday night program was scheduled for early September 1956, but oddly enough both the singer and the host were absent from CBS's New York studio when the time came. In early August, Sullivan was in a serious automobile accident that kept him hospitalized for weeks. He was not personally on hand when Presley appeared.

"If the accident taught me anything," he later said, "it was the value of lining up programs well in advance." Instead, Sullivan hired esteemed British actor Charles Laughton to emcee the show. It was an odd combination in that Laughton's dignified manner and staid British accent was in sharp contrast to what Presley offered. One newspaper called it "The strangest parlay in show business." Sullivan may have chosen Laughton in hopes that the actor's refined sensibilities would offset Presley's wild stage presence and therefore mitigate complaints from some of his more conservative viewers. If Presley was obscene and dangerous as some claimed, then Laughton was his polar opposite. As for Presley, his part of the show was broadcast via remote hookup from a CBS studio in Hollywood, where production had begun on his first film.[69]

Presley's appearance aired on September 9, 1956. The show's other guests were a typical mix of performers including a comedy troupe called the Vagabonds, a team of acrobats, opera singer Dorothy Sarnoff, and the tap dancing duo Conn and Mann. According to published reports, Presley's Hollywood studio audience numbered around 350, with "90 percent of them bobby soxers." Presley appeared twice on Sullivan's national feed. After Laughton introduced him initially, Presley informed America that his appearance on the show was "probably the greatest honor I've ever had in my life." He then launched into "Don't Be Cruel." Next came "Love Me Tender," the title song from his upcoming film. Both performances were tame by Presley standards in that his cavorting on stage was at a minimum, but the girls in the audience screamed as much as usual. He was more animated during his second segment, as if the first two songs had just been a warm-up. He covered Little Richard's "Ready Teddy," and contrary to popular belief, he was not filmed exclusively from only the waist up. Many of his stage movements were in full view of the studio audience in Hollywood and the audience at home. It was not a repeat of his over-the-top performance on the Berle show, but Presley still danced, swiveled his hips, and made faces, eliciting screams from the studio crowd. "With all that eye-popping, neck-thrusting, body-shaking, and funnyface-making, it's a miracle the fellow produced any sound at all," one columnist wrote the next day.[70]

Before he began his final number, Presley thanked Sullivan and reminded viewers that his second appearance on the show would be the fol-

Elvis Presley looks on as his manager, Tom Parker (*left*), talks with television host Ed Sullivan (*right*). CBS/Getty Images.

lowing month. "Mr. Sullivan, we know that somewhere out there, you're [watching]," he said. "All the boys [in the band] and myself, and everybody out here, are looking forward to seeing you back on television." Turning his attention to the audience, he made the tongue-in-cheek remark, "Friends, as a great philosopher once said," and then launched full throttle into "Hound Dog." It was an abbreviated version of the tune, probably because Sullivan thought that it was the singer's most "dangerous" number and it had a history of generating more controversy than the host wanted to deal with. Presley only sang two verses, and it was obvious that someone had instructed the camera operators to concentrate on his upper torso as he performed that particular number. While the gyrations of Presley's legs during Fontana's famous drum fills were out of the camera frame, the screams from the audience, as well as Presley's upper body movements, probably titillated television viewers at home even more than they would have had they been in full view. It was obvious that something was going on down there, but impossible to tell what it was. As a result, those at home were left to their own imaginations.[71]

Reviews of the show were mixed. As always, most older pundits were critical, but some seemed pleased that his stage cavorting had been somewhat restrained, and that cameras captured much of his performance in close up, or from the waist up. "He was most frequently seen in portrait shots," a New York columnist wrote, "and when he wasn't, he jumped about as if someone was giving him a hotfoot. But he didn't act as if he were left over from the burlesque house." Sullivan was reportedly worried about alienating older viewers, but those concerns likely dimmed the next day when newspapers published the overnight ratings summaries. They were explosive. Sullivan's Sunday night program reached 60 million viewers, a staggering 82 percent of the US viewing public at the time. The Trendex ratings service gave his show a 43.7 rating, compared to NBC's 4.2 and ABC's 3.6. In fact, Steve Allen took the night off from his show that week, knowing that Presley's appearance on CBS was a sure winner. "One can't blame Steve Allen for taking last Sunday night off," columnist Kay Gardella opined two days after Sullivan's scorched-earth victory. "Although it wasn't very sporting, it would have been a waste of effort to try to compete against the teenagers' heart throb Elvis Presley."[72]

Presley also performed "Hound Dog" during his second appearance on Sullivan's program, which aired on October 28, 1956, from New York and did not involve a remote hookup. The ratings were not as high as they had been for the first telecast, but they were still powerful, with Sullivan outdrawing his competition for viewers by more than two to one. This show also produced the most authentic of the singer's televised "Hound Dog" performances on Sullivan's show. It was a full version of the song done with intensity, but also with good humor. Presley was more comfortable on the second broadcast. He bantered with the audience and was obviously looser. The way he introduced the song was also a clue as to how he really felt about it. Presley's "Hound Dog" had never been a cover of Big Mama Thornton's version. It was a cover of the Freddie Bell version, which was essentially a parody peppered with musical slapstick. Bell's altered lyrics were ridiculous if not taken tongue-in-cheek, and Presley knew that. As with Bell's take on the song, Presley's "Hound Dog" always had comedic overtones that bordered on being downright silly. Even Presley's bump and grind on the Berle show was supposed to be a joke, although much of the country did not see the humor in it. For this appearance, the audience at home would also see all of the singer—head to toe.[73]

Presley first performed "Love Me Tender" and "Don't Be Cruel." Sullivan then called him out for the final number. Before he started singing, Presley joked with the studio crowd. "I'd like to tell you that we are going to do a sad song for you," he said. "This here song is one of the saddest songs you ever heard. . . ." He then launched into "Hound Dog" with full force. The camera, which started with a relatively tight shot, zoomed out to capture Presley's entire body as he sang, twitched, swiveled, clapped, and grinned his way through the song. It was also obvious that Presley was, at that moment, having a great deal of fun being Elvis Presley, and while he delivered the song with great vigor, he was also not taking himself too seriously. Several times he seemed to stifle a chuckle as he sang. It was a vintage performance, and the audience screamed with delight. Afterward, crowds made it difficult for the singer to leave the building, forcing him to exit through a basement door. Columnist Earl Wilson was with the Presley entourage as they launched their escape. "We all swept down into the basement, under a stage," he later said, "and then to a door leading onto Broadway where some cops, seeing us coming, cleared the way. Elvis pierced the crowd expertly, wriggling out of squealing girls' hands, and dived into a taxicab that shot away."[74]

Presley's final "Hound Dog" performance for Sullivan came on January 6, 1957, during the singer's third appearance on the show. It was another abbreviated version sung as a medley with "Love Me Tender" and "Heartbreak Hotel." The appearance was significant for several reasons. It was the only show where cameramen were told to shoot Presley only from the waist up, orders that would go down in the annals of rock 'n' roll history. While the traditional version of the story holds that Presley fell victim to CBS censors, the situation may have been little more than a publicity stunt. It did not seem particularly logical that, after two previous appearances on the program, Sullivan or CBS would suddenly order a wholesale change in how Presley's segments were produced. If the singer's movement posed a moral threat to the country, why had the "waist up only" order not been in place all along. Despite the camera angles, no one could control the studio audience's reaction when Presley moved around. Females in the studio screamed as Presley gyrated. At home, the audience could not tell what was going on, but the fact that they were forbidden to view it made the performance even more exciting, thus negating anything that censors sought to accomplish. If having Presley filmed only from the waist up was a publicity move, the stunt probably originated in the mind of master huckster Tom Parker, and it was very effective. Presley fans continued to talk about the supposed censorship for years, to the point where most incorrectly believed that the singer was only filmed from the waist up during all of his Sullivan appearances.[75]

Presley's final appearance on the show was also designed, at least somewhat, to help soften his hedonistic image, and in the process broaden his appeal. At the end of the show, Presley's final number was "Peace in the Valley," a popular hymn that was a significant departure from the singer's usual fare. The gospel rendering, which included soft backing vocals from the Jordanaires, was in some ways just as powerful as Presley's popular tunes. After the song ended, Sullivan came out of the wings and unexpectedly conveyed upon the singer a mantle of respectability in front of the American viewing public. "I wanted to say to Elvis Presley and the country that this a real decent, fine boy," he said. "We want to say that we have never had a pleasanter experience on our show with a big name than we've had with you. You are thoroughly alright." Presley shook hands with Sullivan, took a final bow, and left the stage. It was a surprising declaration considering Presley's reputation at the time and Sullivan's place representing the broadcast establishment. Rumors later circulated that Parker had threatened to pull Presley off the show if the host did not say something flattering about the singer. Parker hoped to broaden the singers appeal, and he knew that a positive testimonial from Sullivan would certainly be a good first step along those lines.[76]

Elvis Presley's performances on the *Ed Sullivan Show* marked the end of an era for the singer, and for 1950s rock 'n' roll. The appearances legitimized Presley. It did not destroy his image as rebel, but it softened the rougher edges. The massive exposure took much of the mystery out of what Presley did, much more so than any newspaper account of his stage moves. By his third appearance on the show, viewers knew what to expect. They watched Elvis Presley firsthand and, despite the hoopla, seemed to suffer no lasting ill effects. Ed Sullivan had called him a "decent, fine boy" and some big name journalists started following suit. "I can't believe that Elvis has any wickedness in his heart," famous entertainment columnist Louella Parsons told her readers in another stamp of approval from the establishment. "He is serious about his career." Madison Avenue also took notice, identifying Presley as a vehicle to sell almost anything to a growing teenage market. His fans were loyal, and they purchased everything associated with him. Speaking of the major advertising gurus in New York, one columnist opined that Presley "excites them, but not because of his way with a song or his freewheeling hips. They see Elvis Presley as a way to reach the teenage market. . . . Big advertisers are flocking in, trying to get on the Presley and Associates rock and roll bandwagon." For better or worse, after the Sullivan shows, Presley entered the mainstream.[77]

There are many accounts of the rest of Presley's life. After the Sullivan shows, he continued drawing enthusiastic crowds, but his days as a renegade were numbered. He entered the US Army in 1958, serving in Germany, and was honorably discharged two years later. Upon his return to the United States he received another significant nod from the establishment when Frank Sinatra hosted a television special celebrating the homecoming. Afterward, Presley recorded many songs that appeared on both the pop and country charts in the United States and elsewhere, but for most of the 1960s his career revolved around starring roles in a string of mediocre films designed to sell soundtracks. He remained an icon with millions of fans, but was displaced as an agent of cultural change by younger artists, most famously the Beatles, who arrived in America in 1964 for their own landmark appearance on the *Ed Sullivan Show*. Presley experienced a career revival in 1968, appearing in a highly praised "comeback special" on television, and then conquering Las Vegas. At the time, few could have imagined that he had less than a decade to live. He continued touring during the 1970s but developed a serious addiction to prescription drugs, gained weight, and in general started an unhealthy, downward spiral. He died at Graceland, his home in Memphis, on August 16, 1977, succumbing to his own success as much as anything else. He was forty-two years old.

"Hound Dog" became one of Elvis Presley's most popular recordings, both commercially and in the public mind. It was forever associated with him as a signature song, obscuring to a great degree Willie Mae Thornton's original version, and certainly Freddie Bell's hybrid. It was part of Presley's concert repertoire for the rest of his life. He sang the song onstage for the last time on June 26, 1977, in front of a sold-out crowd at Market Square Arena in Indianapolis, Indiana. His delivery was up-tempo but somewhat garbled during what turned out to be his final show.

For decades since Elvis Presley's 1977 death, fans have scrawled graffiti on the front wall of Graceland, Presley's home in Memphis, including innumerable references to "Hound Dog." Author's collection.

EPILOGUE

"Hound Dog"... When I heard it, it just shot straight through to my brain.
I realized, suddenly, that there was more to life
than what I'd been living.

—**BRUCE SPRINGSTEEN,** BBC Radio, 2016

Elvis Presley's version of "Hound Dog" was a global hit and an essential part of the American soundtrack of the 1950s and beyond. Once he released it, the song belonged to the world, and it became one of the most covered rock 'n' roll tunes of all time. Through the years hundreds of artists covered Presley's version or added it to their stage acts. It was easy to play, easy to dance to, and there were not a lot of complicated lyrics to memorize. The first line of the song also provided a great hook. Even some of Presley's contemporaries got involved. "Little Richard" Penniman, who many consider the real king of rock 'n' roll, recorded a version, as did the Everly Brothers, Tom Jones, and Carl Perkins. Jerry Lee Lewis covered the song, but only after recording a version with Leiber and Stoller's original lyrics. Pat Boone recorded an entire album of Presley songs in 1963, including a syrupy and decidedly nonthreatening "Hound Dog."

Of the early retreads, a handful stood out. Three African American artists were quick to cover the Presley hit, following essentially the same rhythm and using the Freddie Bell lyrics. Benjamin Sherman "Scatman" Crothers was a guitarist, drummer, and actor who led his own band for years in New York and Los Angeles. His 1956 cover of the Presley version was likely the first one produced. Bandleader, saxophonist, and harmonica player Buddy Lucas recorded a version around the same time, as did Jimmy Witherspoon, an R&B

singer who could be a rocker when the mood struck him. In 1961, June Dyer, a South African vocalist, became the first white female to record Presley's version of song, and three years later the Surfaris, who had a big hit in the 1960s with "Wipe Out," recorded a version of "Hound Dog" using a general surf rock template recently popularized by Dick Dale and the Beach Boys.

As a key member of rock 'n' roll's founding generation, Elvis Presley was obviously a great influence on everything in the genre that came later. The rock legends who dominated the 1960s idolized Presley, routinely crediting him with charting the course for their own careers. "When I first heard Elvis Presley's voice," Bob Dylan once said, "I just knew that I wasn't going to work for anybody and nobody was going to be my boss. Hearing him for the first time was like busting out of jail." In England and Hamburg, Germany, the earliest Beatles club shows reportedly included covers of "Hound Dog." Much later, in 1972, John Lennon performed the song live at a benefit concert at Madison Square Garden in New York, at one point blurting out "Elvis, I love ya" as he sang. This version was included on Lennon's *Live in New York City* album, released posthumously in 1986. Jimi Hendrix recorded his take on "Hound Dog" while appearing on BBC radio in Britain in 1967, and it eventually appeared on the 1998 MCA release *The Jimi Hendrix Experience: BBC Sessions.* Just a year after Presley's 1977 death, the Rolling Stones visited Memphis while touring in support of their new album *Some Girls,* opening their show with a rousing version of "Hound Dog" as an homage to the city's most famous resident. The trend continued into the twenty-first century, and a seemingly endless string of cover versions of Elvis Presley's "Hound Dog" have been released, including a number of instrumentals.

Like Presley himself, "Hound Dog" was popular in overseas markets, spawning the occasional foreign language cover. Popular German singer Ralf Bendix sang one of the first in 1957. His rendering had altered lyrics but kept the original melody, and included attempts to replicate D. J. Fontana's drum fills and Scotty Moore's solo. Austrian jazz composer Johannes Fehring also recorded a version that same year. In the early 1960s, Dino Y Los Solitarios and Los Rogers recorded versions in Spanish, and French singer Lucky Blondo's 1977 "Hound Dog" was recorded in Nashville with backing vocals by the Jordanaires. The Japanese band Hound Dog, whose name was an homage to Presley's recording, toured extensively and had a number of hits in their home country during the 1980s and 1990s. In 1984, Angela Ro Ro recorded a piano-centered version of "Hound Dog" sung in Portuguese, and several years later Zuri West produced yet another German version. As with the American offerings, foreign versions of the song have been many and varied through the years.

The success of Elvis Presley's "Hound Dog" overshadowed but did not erase the impact of Big Mama Thornton's original recording. The great blues revival of the late 1950s and 1960s, which was entangled with the rise of rock 'n' roll, led many young people to seek out the blues artists who influenced contemporary rock, and whose work had been obscured by the segregated society in which they lived. This included Thornton, whose legacy as the first artist to record "Hound Dog" became more widely recognized as the years passed. This led to more covers of her version, by artists Black and white, using the original melody and the Leiber and Stoller lyrics. Soul singer Betty Everett recorded a 1963 version of the Thornton classic, as did Junior Wells' Chicago Blues Band two years later. In 1967, the Dirty Blues Band, a collection of white musicians from California, produced a version of Thornton's song, and in 1989 Eric Clapton included a cover on his album *Journeyman*. Other notables who followed Thornton's lead on the song were Etta James in 2000, Macy Gray in 2004, and Dee Dee Bridgewater in 2017.

On the surface, "Hound Dog" is a song that seems to have little depth of meaning. The Presley version especially is a nonsensical number. It tells no cohesive story, and the melody is simple and repetitive. The Big Mama Thornton original is much better from a musical standpoint, but even so, its theme involving the complicated relationship between men and women is ancient and oft told. As an artistic statement, Freddie Bell's version is forgettable, as are most of the covers and answers to the more popular renderings. All that said, if one takes these individual versions of the song and looks at them collectively as an evolutionary story of a piece of music, a quintessential American tale emerges. "Hound Dog" becomes an enduring statement of American multiculturalism, both silly and serious. Two male, Jewish teenagers from the North, who were living in California and seemed to enjoy pretending they were Black, penned the number specifically for an African American woman from the South, and the song resonated with Black audiences. It was a decently crafted blues tune filtered through the minds of two white kids. That concept alone is enough to provoke a generous amount of discussion, even before considering Presley's later version.

The fact that Freddie Bell served as the catalyst for Presley's "Hound Dog" offered an unusual twist to the story. Ironically, Presley, a rhythm and blues devotee, decided to record the song not after hearing the gritty original by Big Mama Thornton, but after hearing Bell's interpretation, which had different lyrics, a different rhythm, and was presented as a novelty number. At the time, not even Presley himself could have imagined that "Hound Dog" would become his signature tune. Once the song hit for him, its enormity generated not only lawsuits but discussions about cultural appropriation. Along those lines, Leiber and Stoller through the years maintained their writing credit, while the argument that Presley "stole" the song from Thornton is complicated by Leiber, Stoller, and Freddie Bell's presence in the song's narrative. Despite her stellar interpretation of the tune, Thornton did not write "Hound Dog," and Presley's hit was actually a cover of Bell's version, which was quite different from Thornton's. Some purists might also argue that Thornton's version was not an authentic blues song in the first place because two white kids wrote it. Hence, the discourse over who stole what from who, and what is authentic and what is not, can spin completely out of control.

Almost all of the original players in the "Hound Dog" drama are gone. Elvis Presley famously passed away in Memphis in 1977, while Willie Mae Thornton died in Los Angeles in 1984. Leiber and Stoller as a team went on to have a prolific songwriting career, composing many memorable tunes, including "Jailhouse Rock" and several other hits for Presley, and a string of successful records for the Coasters, the Drifters, Ben E. King, and many others. Leiber died in Los Angeles in 2011, but Mike Stoller is still among the living in his nineties. After a long and fruitful music career that landed him in the Rock and Roll Hall of Fame, Johnny Otis died in 2012, and the irascible, overbearing Don Robey left us back in 1975. Sam Phillips, whose later association with Presley made him a legendary character in the music business, passed away in 2003. Rufus Thomas remained one of the most beloved figures in the history of Memphis entertainment, and upon his death in 2001 the whole city went into mourning. After a long, steady career in Las Vegas, Freddie Bell passed away there in 2008, with his role in the "Hound Dog" story still relatively unrecognized.

Like rock 'n' roll itself, there is a duality to "Hound Dog." The song is both simple and complicated at the same time. There were heavy racial components and gender issues in play throughout its evolution, written as it was by two white, Jewish males for a Black female, and later popularized by another white male who sounded Black. In typical American fashion, its success spawned lawsuits as everyone involved in the song's creation (and some who were not) jockeyed for a piece of the financial pie. It also represented a generational changing of the guard, cementing Elvis Presley's reputation as a superstar who was much more than a passing fad. "It was the song in which he told the world: rock and roll is here to stay," *Rolling Stone* magazine claimed in 2004 while citing the song on its list of the five hundred greatest songs of all time. "Presley transformed the song's blues changes and put-down rhyme into a declaration of independence from one generation to its cold, rigid elders."[1]

Now, many years later, those kids who broke ranks with their "cold, rigid elders" are elderly themselves, if they are still around at all. Far from inflammatory, the rebellious rock 'n' roll music that they listened to in their youth has been relegated the stuff of deep nostalgia. To modern teenagers it is ancient. The blues and R&B music that white parents once feared became mainstream long ago, and instead of turning it off, many white "grown ups" now turn it up when they hear it. If they were good to begin with, the old songs certainly hold up, but the abject danger that they once represented is gone. Today, neither Big Mama Thornton's or Elvis Presley's versions of "Hound Dog" receive much airplay, or inspire many purchases, and most of the other renderings of the song have been dead and buried for decades. That said, "Hound Dog" is still a significant piece of Americana, and an important milestone in the history of popular music. It has incredible staying power in that it evolved over time from something groundbreaking to something historic. It is evocative of a particular era, but the racial, gender, and generational issues that were part of its creation are still relevant today in other forms. As a result, the song remains what it always has been, a simple, silly ditty that had serious consequences.

APPENDIX

Covering "Hound Dog"

"Hound Dog" has been covered hundreds of times since the issue of Big Mama Thornton's original version in 1953. Below is a selected list of artists who recorded covers of the Thornton or Presley versions, along with artists who recorded parody or answer songs.

Willie Mae "Big Mama" Thornton Version

Willie Mae "Big Mama" Thornton (1953)
Little Esther (1953)
Jack Turner and His Granger County Gang (1953)
Billy Starr (1953)
Betsy Gay (1953)
Eddie Hazlewood (1953)
Tommy Duncan and the Miller Bros. (1953)
Cleve Jackson and His Hound Dogs (1953)
Junior Wells (1965)
Jeanette Williams (1967)
The Dirty Blues Band (1967)
James Booker (1982)
Susan Tedeschi (1995)
Etta James (2000)
Robert Palmer (2003)
Macy Gray (2004, live recording)
Beverley Knight, featuring Jools Holland (2016)
Dee Dee Bridgewater (2017)

Elvis Presley Version

Freddie Bell and the Bellboys (1955)
Elvis Presley (1956)
Gene Vincent and His Blue Caps (1956)
Jerry Lee Lewis (1958)
Chubby Checker (1961)
Pat Boone (1963)
Sammy Davis Jr. (1963, live recording)
Betty Everett (1963)
Little Richard (1964)
The Surfaris (1964)
The Everly Brothers (1965)
The Mothers of Invention (1967, live recording)
Jimi Hendrix (1967)
Vanilla Fudge (1968)
Van Morrison (1971, live recording)
Conway Twitty (1972)
John Lennon (1972, live recording)
John Entwistle (1973)
The Rolling Stones (1978, live recording)
Scorpions (1978, live recording)
Carl Perkins (1985)
Eric Clapton (1989)
Tiny Tim (1993)
David Grisman, John Hartford, and Mike Seeger (1999)
James Taylor (2008)
Robin Trower (2013)
Steve Tyrell, featuring Chuck Leavell (2015)

Answers and Parody Versions

Charlie Gore and Louis Innis, "You Ain't Nothin' but a Female Hound Dog" (1953)

Homer and Jethro, “How Much Is That Hound Dog in the Window?” (1953)
Roy Brown and His Mighty, Mighty Men, “Mr. Hound Dog’s in Town” (1953)
John Brim, “Rattlesnake” (1953)
Chuck Higgins and His Mellotones, “Real Gone Hound Dog” (1953)
Smiley Lewis, “Play Girl” (1953)
Rufus “Hound Dog” Thomas Jr., “Bear Cat (The Answer to Hound Dog)” (1953)
Juanita Moore and the Eugene Jackson Trio, “Call Me a Hound Dog” (1953)
Frank “Dual Trumpeter” Motley and His Crew, “New Hound Dog” (1954)
Big Tiny Kennedy and His Orchestra, “Country Boy” (1955)
Homer and Jethro, “Houn’ Dawg” (1956)
Lalo “Pancho Lopez” Guerrero, “Pound Dog” (1956)
Cliff Johnson, “Go ’Way Hound Dog (Let Me Sing My Blues)” (1956)
Mickey Katz and His Orchestra, “You’re a Doity Dog” (1957)
Johnny Madera, “Too Many Hound Dogs” (1960)
The Raging Storms, “Hound Dog Twist” (1961)

Notes

1. The Songwriters

1. United States, *WWII Draft Cards, Young Men, 1940–1947* (on-line database), Ancestry.com (accessed June 1, 2020); United States Census, 1910, Bronx Assembly District 32, New York, New York; United States Social Security Administration, *Social Security Death Index, Master File,* United States Social Security Administration; Washington D.C.; United States Census, 1940, New York, Queens, New York; David Samuels, "Rhythm and Jews," *Tablet,* June 12, 2016, https://www.tabletmag.com/sections/arts-letters/articles/rhythm-and-jews (accessed June 10, 2020); *Altoona (Pa.) Tribune,* April 19, 1923; *New York Daily News,* March 25, 1928.

2. *Freehold (N.J.) Transcript and Monmouth Inquirer,* January 26, 1940; *Topanga (Calif.) Journal,* May 18, 1951; *Brooklyn (N.Y.) Eagle,* December 1, 1946; Jerry Leiber and Mike Stoller, with David Ritz, *Hound Dog: The Leiber and Stoller Autobiography* (New York: Simon and Schuster, 2009), 4–5.

3. David Samuels, "Rhythm and Jews," *Tablet,* June 12, 2016, https://www.tabletmag.com/sections/arts-letters/articles/rhythm-and-jews (accessed June 10, 2020).

4. William C. Banfield, *Black Notes: Essays of a Musician Writing in the Post-Album Age* (Lanham, Md.: Scarecrow Press, 2004), 165–179; *New York Times,* April 21, 2020; *Wall Street Journal,* May 28, 2012.

5. Jerry Leiber and Mike Stoller, with David Ritz, *Hound Dog: The Leiber and Stoller Autobiography,* 8–9, 17–18; *New York Daily News,* September 26, 1947. David Griffiths, *Hot Jazz: From Harlem to Storyville* (Lanham, Md.: Scarecrow Press, 1998), 214; Bill Kirchner, ed. *The Oxford Companion to Jazz* (New York: Oxford Univ. Press, 2000), 725–726; For a detailed treatment of New York's 52nd Street and its place in entertainment history, see Arnold Shaw, *52nd Street: The Street of Jazz* (Boston, Mass.: Da Capo, 1977).

6. Jerry Leiber and Mike Stoller, with David Ritz, *Hound Dog: The Leiber and Stoller Autobiography,* 17–18; George Lipsitz, *Time Passages: Collective Memory and American Popular Culture* (Minneapolis: Univ. of Minnesota Press, 1990), 140; Frances R. Aparicio and Candida F. Jaquez, eds. *Musical Migrations: Transnationalism and Cultural Hybridity in Latino America,* vol. 1 (New York: Palgrave Macmillan, 2003), 187.

7. Jerry Leiber and Mike Stoller, with David Ritz, *Hound Dog: The Leiber and Stoller Autobiography,* 24–29; Frances R. Aparicio and Candida F. Jaquez, eds. *Musical Migrations: Transnationalism and Cultural Hybridity in Latino America,* vol. 1, 187; Robert Palmer, *Baby, That Was Rock & Roll: The Legendary Leiber and Stoller* (New York: Harcourt Brace Jovanovich, 1978), 16.

8. United States Census, 1940, Baltimore, Baltimore City, Maryland; R. L. Polk and Company, *Baltimore City Directory, 1930* (Detroit, Mich.: R. L. Polk, 1930), 1744; Joe Smith and Jerry Leiber. *Off the Record Interview with Jerry Leiber, (1988?),* audio recording, Library of Congress, Washington, D.C., https://www.loc.gov/item/jsmith000110/ ((accessed June 1, 2020).

9. Jerry Leiber and Mike Stoller, with David Ritz, *Hound Dog: The Leiber and Stoller Autobiography,* 7; Joe Smith and Jerry Leiber, *Off the Record Interview with Jerry Leiber, (1988?).*

10. Joe Smith and Jerry Leiber, *Off the Record Interview with Jerry Leiber, (1988?).*

11. *Baltimore (Md.) Sun,* February 4, 1992; Michael Olesker, *Front Stoops in the Fifties: Baltimore Legends Come of Age* (Baltimore, Md.: John Hopkins Univ. Press, 2013), 30–31; Jerry Leiber and Mike Stoller, with David Ritz, *Hound Dog: The Leiber and Stoller Autobiography,* 2–3.

12. *Baltimore (Md.) Sun,* December 8, 1996; Joe Smith and Jerry Leiber. *Off the Record Interview with Jerry Leiber, (1988?).*

13. *Baltimore (Md.) Sun,* December 8, 1996; *North Hollywood (Calif.) Valley Times,* January 30, 1956; *Los Angeles Times,* December 13, 1998; California Department of Public Health, County Birth, Marriage, and Death Records, 1830–1980; Jerry Leiber and Mike Stoller, with David Ritz, *Hound Dog: The Leiber and Stoller Autobiography,* 25–28.

14. *Baltimore (Md.) Sun,* December 8, 1996; *Los Angeles Times,* August 11, 2004; *Pasadena (Calif.) Independent,* August 9, 1951: *Chicago Tribune,* August 14, 2004; Barney Hoskyns, *Waiting for the Sun: A Rock 'n' Roll History of Los Angeles* (Milwaukee, Wisc.: Backbeat Books, 1996), 35.

15. "Rock and Roll; In The Groove; *Interview with Jerry Leiber and Mike Stoller* [Part 1 of 7]," WGBH Media Library and Archives, http://openvault.wgbh.org/catalog/V_3B7201E645E8476797EB49ECC8B901C1 (accessed May 30, 2020).

16. *Los Angeles Times,* February 2, 1997, August 18, 2005; Josh Alan Friedman, *Tell the Truth Until They Bleed: Coming Clean in the Dirty World of Blues and Rock 'n' Roll* (Milwaukee, Wisc.: Backbeat Books, 2008), 43.

17. John Broven, *Record Makers and Breakers: Voices of Independent Rock 'n' Roll Pioneers* (Champaign: Univ. of Illinois Press, 2009), 39–44; Joe Smith and Lester Sill, *Off the Record Interview with Lester Sill, 1986-03-13,* audio recording, Library of Congress, Washington, D.C., https://www.loc.gov/item/jsmith000138/ (accessed June 6, 2020).

18. Jerry Leiber and Mike Stoller, with David Ritz, *Hound Dog: The Leiber and Stoller Autobiography,* 28–31.

19. Joe Smith and Lester Sill, *Off the Record Interview with Lester Sill, 1986-03-13.*

20. "Rock and Roll; In The Groove; *Interview with Jerry Leiber and Mike Stoller* [Part 1 of 7]"; Paul Zollo, *More Songwriters on Songwriting* (Boston, Mass.: Da Capo, 2016), 11–20.

21. *Baltimore (Md.) Sun,* December 8, 1996; *New Musical Express,* February 15, 1975; Bill Boggs, Jerry Leiber, and Mike Stoller, *Jerry Leiber and Mike Stoller Full Interview with Bill*

Boggs, BillBoggsTV, https://www.youtube.com/watch?v=v2UU-GuNOIo (accessed June 5, 2020); Richard Aquila, *Let's Rock: How 1950s America Created Elvis and the Rock and Roll Craze* (New York: Rowman and Littlefield, 2017), 234–235.

22. *Ithaca (N.Y.) Journal,* June 13, 1957; Joe Smith and Jerry Leiber. *Off the Record Interview with Jerry Leiber, (1988?)*; Joe Smith and Lester Sill, *Off the Record Interview with Lester Sill, 1986-03-13.*

23. David Fricke, "Leiber and Stoller: *Rolling Stone*'s 1990 Interview with the Songwriting Legends," *Rolling Stone,* August 22, 2011, https://www.rollingstone.com/music/music-news/leiber-and-stoller-rolling-stones-1990-interview-with-the-songwriting-legends-246405/ (accessed June 11, 2020).

24. Joe Smith and Lester Sill, *Off the Record Interview with Lester Sill, 1986-03-13*; Jerry Leiber and Mike Stoller, with David Ritz, *Hound Dog: The Leiber and Stoller Autobiography,* 37–39. Theo Cateforis, ed., *The Rock History Reader* (New York: Routledge, 2007), 32–33.

25. Michael Campbell, *Popular Music in America: The Beat Goes On,* 4th ed. (Boston, Mass.: Schirmer Cengage Learning, 2013), 186–187; Ken Emerson, *Always Magic in the Air: The Bomp and Brilliance of the Brill Building Era* (London: Fourth Estate, 2006) 12–18.

26. Tony Russell, *The Blues: From Robert Johnson to Robert Cray.* (London: Aurum, 1997), 13; *New Musical Express,* February 15, 1975.

27. Hank Bordowitz, *Dirty Little Secrets of the Record Business* (Chicago: Chicago Review Press, 2007), 31, 298–300; John Broven, *Record Makers and Breakers: Voices of Independent Rock 'n' Roll Pioneers,* 299; Robert L. Eagle and Eric S. LeBlanc, *Blues: A Regional Experience* (Santa Barbara, Calif.: Praeger, 2013), 353.

28. Jerry Leiber and Mike Stoller, with David Ritz, *Hound Dog: The Leiber and Stoller Autobiography,* 38; Michael Lydon, *Ray Charles: Man and Music* (New York: Routledge, 2004), 36–37.

29. David Fricke, "Leiber and Stoller: *Rolling Stone*'s 1990 Interview with the Songwriting Legends."

30. Jerry Leiber and Mike Stoller, with David Ritz, *Hound Dog: The Leiber and Stoller Autobiography,* 45–46. Sean J. O'Connell, *Images of America: Los Angeles's Central Avenue Jazz* (Charleston, S.C.: Arcadia, 2014), 7–9. For a detailed treatment of Central Avenue's place in African American history and music history, see R. J. Smith, *The Great Black Way: L.A. in the 1940s and the Lost African American Renaissance* (New York: PublicAffairs, 2006). *Billboard,* May 15, 1961.

31. John Hartley Fox, *King of the Queen City: The Story of King Records* (Champaign: Univ. of Illinois Press, 2009), 86–87.

32. Jerry Leiber and Mike Stoller, with David Ritz, *Hound Dog: The Leiber and Stoller Autobiography,* 57–59.

33. *Billboard,* October 8, 1949; Marc Myers, *Anatomy of a Song: The Oral History of 45 Iconic Hits That Changed Rock, R&B and Pop* (New York: Grove Press, 2016), 14–18.

34. David Fricke, "Leiber and Stoller: *Rolling Stone*'s 1990 Interview with the Songwriting Legends"; Marc Myers, *Anatomy of a Song: The Oral History of 45 Iconic Hits That Changed Rock, R&B and Pop,* 14–18; Theo Cateforis, ed., *The Rock History Reader,* 27.

35. *Billboard*, March 30, 1959.

36. Robert Palmer, *Baby, That Was Rock & Roll: The Legendary Leiber and Stoller*, 20.

2. Big Mama

1. United States Census, 1930, Alameda, Berkeley, California; *Washington Post*, June 24, 1985; United States, *World War I Draft Registration Cards, 1917–1918* (on-line database), Ancestry.com (accessed June 10, 2020); George Lipsitz, *Midnight at the Barrelhouse: The Johnny Otis Story* (Minneapolis: Univ. of Minnesota Press, 2010), 9; Brian D. Behnken, *The Struggle in Black and Brown: African American and Mexican American Relations During the Civil Rights Era* (Lincoln: Univ. of Nebraska Press, 2011), 218; Johnny Otis, *Listen to the Lambs* (New York: Norton, 1968), xxxv; *Los Angeles Times*, July 7, 1968; Terry Gross and Johnny Otis, *Fresh Air with Terry Gross: Interview with Johnny Otis*, National Public Radio, WHYY Public Media, Philadelphia, Pennsylvania, original air date November 21, 1989.

2. *Roseville (Calif.) Press-Tribune*, October 27, 1939; *San Francisco Examiner*, October 18, 1939; *Oakland Tribune*, October 15, 1939; George Lipsitz, *Midnight at the Barrelhouse: The Johnny Otis Story*, 9.

3. United States Census, 1920, Alameda, Oakland, California; United States Census, 1940, Alameda, Oakland, California; California Department of Health Services, *California Birth Index, 1905–1995*, California Department of Health Services, Center for Health Statistics, Sacramento, California; United States, *World War I Draft Registration Cards, 1917–1918* (on-line database), Ancestry.com (accessed June 10, 2020); Harris County, Texas, Marriage Records, Harris County Clerk's Office, Houston, Texas; *San Francisco Examiner*, June 26, 1983.

4. Frank Driggs and Chuck Haddix, *Kansas City Jazz: From Ragtime to Bebop—A History* (New York: Oxford Univ. Press, 2005), 64; Preston Love, *A Thousand Honey Creeks Later: My Life in Music, from Basie to Motown—and Beyond* (Middletown, Conn.: Wesleyan Univ. Press, 1997), 54; George Lipsitz, *Midnight at the Barrelhouse: The Johnny Otis Story*, 19; Terry Gross and Johnny Otis, *Fresh Air with Terry Gross: Interview with Johnny Otis.*

5. *San Francisco Examiner*, June 26, 1983; Johnny Otis, *Upside Your Head: Rhythm and Blues on Central Avenue* (Hanover, N.H.: Univ. Press of New England, 1993), 38.

6. George Lipsitz, *Midnight at the Barrelhouse: The Johnny Otis Story*, 54–55; *Saint George (Utah) Daily Spectrum*, August 10, 1988; Charlie Gillett and Johnny Otis, *Interview with Johnny Otis* (1970), http://www.rocksbackpages.com/Library/Article/johnny-otis-1970 (accessed June 26, 2020).

7. George Lipsitz, *Midnight at the Barrelhouse: The Johnny Otis Story*, 54–55; *Saint George (Utah) Daily Spectrum*, August 10, 1988; Charlie Gillett and Johnny Otis, *Interview with Johnny Otis* (1970); Johnny Otis, *Upside Your Head: Rhythm and Blues on Central Avenue*, 46.

8. *Saint George (Utah) Daily Spectrum*, August 10, 1988; Charlie Gillett and Johnny Otis, *Interview with Johnny Otis* (1970).

9. *Pittsburgh (Pa.) Courier*, March 25, 1950, May 19, 1951; Bill Greensmith, Mike Rowe, and Mark Camarigg, eds., *Blues Unlimited: Essential Interviews from the Original Blues Magazine* (Chicago: Univ. of Illinois Press, 2015), 424–425.

10. Preston Lauterbach, "Sympathy for the Devil," *Oxford American* 87 (winter 2014), https://www.oxfordamerican.org/magazine/item/1040-sympathy-for-the-devil#:~:text=By%2019 40%2C%20Robey%20routinely%20booked,Duke%20Ellington%20and%20Ella%20Fitzgerald (accessed July 14, 2020); James M. Salem, *The Late Great Johnny Ace and the Transition from R&B to Rock 'n' Roll* (Urbana, Ill.: Univ. of Chicago Press, 1999), 53–54; Josh Alan Friedman, *Tell the Truth Until They Bleed: Coming Clean in the Dirty World of Blues and Rock 'n' Roll,* 18–21.

11. Charles Farley, *Soul of the Man: Bobby "Blue" Bland* (Jackson: Univ. Press of Mississippi, 2011), 54; Tyina L. Steptoe, *Houston Bound: Culture and Color in a Jim Crow City* (Berkeley: Univ. of California Press, 2015), 192.

12. Charles Farley, *Soul of the Man: Bobby "Blue" Bland,* 61; Nelson George, *The Death of Rhythm & Blues* (New York: Penguin, 1988), 58–59.

13. Nelson George, *The Death of Rhythm & Blues,* 58–59; Grady Gaines, with Rod Evans, *I've Been Out There: On the Road with Legends of Rock 'n' Roll* (College Station: Texas A&M Univ. Press, 2015), 33–34; Charles White: *The Life and Times of Little Richard: The Authorized Biography* (London, UK: Omnibus Press, 1984), 37; Bill Greensmith, Mike Rowe, and Mark Camarigg, eds., *Blues Unlimited: Essential Interviews from the Original Blues Magazine,* 352.

14. *Houston Chronicle,* April 15, 2011; Josh Alan Friedman, *Tell the Truth Until They Bleed: Coming Clean in the Dirty World of Blues and Rock 'n' Roll,* 18–21.

15. *Fort Worth (Tex.) Star-Telegram,* May 13, 2001.

16. Chris Strachwitz and Willie Mae Thornton, *Big Mama Thornton Interview* (date unknown), The Chris Strachwitz Collection, Arhoolie Foundation, https://arhoolie.org/big-mama-thornton-interview/ (accessed January 5, 2022).

17. *Anniston (Ala.) Star,* October 30, 1946.

18. *San Francisco Examiner,* March 22, 1970.

19. Michael Spörke, *Big Mama Thornton: The Life and Music* (Jefferson, N.C.: McFarland, 2014), 7; Timothy J. O'Brien and David Ensminger, *Mojo Hand: The Life and Music of Lightnin' Hopkins* (Austin: Univ. of Texas Press, 2013), 50–51; *Los Angeles Times,* July 28, 1984.

20. Michael Spörke, *Big Mama Thornton: The Life and Music,* 13–15.

21. *Houston Chronicle,* April 7, 2020.

22. James M. Salem, *The Late Great Johnny Ace and the Transition from R&B to Rock 'n' Roll,* 79–80.

23. David McGee, *B.B. King: There Is Always One More Time* (San Francisco: Backbeat Books, 2005), 78–79. *Billboard,* December 29, 1951.

24. Steve Roeser and Johnny Otis. "Interview with Johnny Otis" (1990), http://www.rocksbackpages.com/Library/Article/johnny-otis-1990 (accessed July 21, 2020).

25. *New York Age,* April 26, 1952.

26. *Honolulu (Hawaii) Star-Bulletin,* January 10, 1965; *Pittsburgh (Pa.) Courier,* August 7, 1965; *San Francisco Chronicle,* April 6, 1970.

27. *Pittsburgh (Pa.) Courier,* August 30, 1952.

28. Steve Roeser and Johnny Otis. "Interview with Johnny Otis" (1990), http://www.rocksbackpages.com/Library/Article/johnny-otis-1990 (accessed July 21, 2020).

29. Bill Millar, "Leiber and Stoller Part One: The Blues (1950–1953)," *Let It Rock* (1974), http://www.rocksbackpages.com/Library/Article/leiber-and-stoller-part-one-the-blues-1950-1953 (accessed August 10, 2020); Steve Roeser and Johnny Otis. "Interview with Johnny Otis" (1990), http://www.rocksbackpages.com/Library/Article/johnny-otis-1990 (accessed July 21, 2020).

30. Jerry Leiber and Mike Stoller, with David Ritz, *Hound Dog: The Leiber and Stoller Autobiography,* 61; David Fricke, "Leiber and Stoller: *Rolling Stone*'s 1990 Interview with the Songwriting Legends."

31. Paul Leslie and Mike Stoller, interview with Mike Stoller, *The Paul Leslie Hour,* http://www.thepaulleslie.com/tag/mike-stoller/ (accessed August 1, 2020); David Fricke, "Leiber and Stoller: *Rolling Stone*'s 1990 Interview with the Songwriting Legends"; Michael Spörke, *Big Mama Thornton: The Life and Music,* 25.

32. Paul Zollo, *More Songwriters on Songwriting,* 11–20.

33. Michael Spörke, *Big Mama Thornton: The Life and Music,* 25.

34. *Philadelphia Enquirer,* September 23, 1988.

35. Jud Hurd, *Cartoon Success Secrets: A Tribute to 35 Years of Cartoonist Profiles* (Kansas City, Mo.: Andrews McMeel Publishing, 2004), 29: Johnny Otis, "Rock and Roll Hall of Fame Induction Speech," 1994, https://www.youtube.com/watch?v=iLiRK40fC8E (accessed August 7, 2020); Paul Leslie and Mike Stoller, interview with Mike Stoller, *The Paul Leslie Hour,* http://www.thepaulleslie.com/tag/mike-stoller/ (accessed August 1, 2020); Edward Komara and Peter Lee, eds., *The Blues Encyclopedia* (New York: Routledge, 2004), 839.

36. Jerry Leiber and Mike Stoller, with David Ritz, *Hound Dog: The Leiber and Stoller Autobiography,* 65; Paul Leslie and Mike Stoller, interview with Mike Stoller, *The Paul Leslie Hour,* http://www.thepaulleslie.com/tag/mike-stoller/ (accessed August 1, 2020).

37. Michael Spörke, *Big Mama Thornton: The Life and Music,* 25–26.

38. United States District Court S.D. New York, *Valjo Music Publishing Corporation, Plaintiff v. Elvis Presley Music, Inc., Mike Stoller and Jerry Leiber, Defendants,* December 4, 1957; Charlie Gillett and Johnny Otis, *Interview with Johnny Otis* (1970).

39. Library of Congress, *Catalogue of Copyright Entries: Unpublished Music, Jan.—June, 1952,* third series, vol. 6, part 5b, N. 1 (Washington, D.C.: Library of Congress, 1953), 508; Jerry Leiber and Mike Stoller, with David Ritz, *Hound Dog: The Leiber and Stoller Autobiography,* 67.

40. George Lipsitz, *Midnight at the Barrelhouse: The Johnny Otis Story,* 43; Charlie Gillett and Johnny Otis, *Interview with Johnny Otis* (1970).

41. David Burke, "Big Mama Thornton: Big Mama's Blues." *Vintage Rock* (2017), http://www.rocksbackpages.com/Library/Article/big-mama-thornton-big-mamas-blues (accessed August 24, 2020); *New York Age,* April 24, 1954.

42. Michael Spörke, *Big Mama Thornton: The Life and Music,* 25–34.

43. Michael Spörke, *Big Mama Thornton: The Life and Music,* 33–36; David Burke, "Big Mama Thornton: Big Mama's Blues." *Vintage Rock* (2017), Rocksbackpages.com; *Philadelphia Enquirer,* August 2, 1984.

3. Answers and Pretenders

1. Michel Ruppli, comp., *The King Labels: A Discography,* vol. 2 (Westport, Conn.: Greenwood Press, 1985), 605–607.

2. *Franklin (Ind.) Evening Star,* June 3, 1944; *Muncie (Ind.) Star Press,* February 23, 1944, June 13, 1944; *Hagerstown (Md.) Morning Call,* August 28, 1954; *El Paso (Tex.) Times,* July 16, 1950.

3. Larry Birnbaum, *Before Elvis: The Pre-History of Rock 'n' Roll* (Lanham, Md.: Scarecrow Press, 2013), 234, 78; *Billboard,* April 4, 1953, 28.

4. Ben Wynne, *In Tune: Charley Patton, Jimmie Rodgers and the Roots of American Music* (Baton Rouge: Louisiana State Univ. Press, 2014), 172; Rachael Rubin and Jeffrey Melnick, eds., *American Popular Music: New Approaches to the 20th Century* (Amherst: Univ. of Massachusetts Press, 2001), 50; Michael Erlewine, Vladimir Bogdanov, Chris Woodstra, and Stephen Thomas Erlewine, eds., *All Music Guide to Country: The Experts' Guide to the Best Recordings in Country Music* (San Francisco: Miller Freeman Books, 2003), 217–218; Discogs, "Jack Turner and His Granger County Gang," https://www.discogs.com/artist/1676181-Jack-Turner-And-His-Granger-County-Gang (accessed July 15, 2021).

5. *Billboard,* December 1, 1951, November 15, 1952; Frank Hoffman, ed., *Encyclopedia of Recorded Sound,* vol. 1 (New York: Routledge, 2005), 33–34; Galen Gart, ed., *First Pressings: A History of Rhythm and Blues,* vol. 3 (Charlottesville: Univ. of Virginia Press, 1986), 40; *Charlotte (N.C.) Observer,* July 8, 1951.

6. *Oklahoma City (Okla.) Daily Oklahoman,* April 19, 1953; Charles R. Townshend, *San Antonio Rose: The Life and Music of Bob Wills* (Urbana: Univ. of Illinois Press, 1976), 57.

7. Michael Erlewine, Vladimir Bogdanov, Chris Woodstra, Stephen Thomas Erlewine, Eds., *All Music Guide to Country: The Experts' Guide to the Best Recordings in Country Music,* 234; Bob Leszczak, *Who Did It First?: Great Rhythm and Blues Cover Songs and Their Original Artists* (Langham, Md.: Scarecrow Press, 2013), 88–89.

8. Josh Alan Friedman, *Tell the Truth Until They Bleed: Coming Clean in the Dirty World of Blues and Rock 'n' Roll,* 21; Larry Birnbaum, *Before Elvis: The Pre-History of Rock 'n' Roll,* 234–235.

9. Josh Alan Friedman, *Tell the Truth Until They Bleed: Coming Clean in the Dirty World of Blues and Rock 'n' Roll,* 21; *Billboard,* April 18, 1953, 48.

10. Larry Birnbaum, *Before Elvis: The Pre-History of Rock 'n' Roll,* 234; *Billboard,* May 23, 1953, 162.

11. Steven Sharp, "John Brim: The Ice Cream Man," *Living Blues* 118 (December 1994), 39–45.

12. Steven Sharp, "John Brim: The Ice Cream Man," 38–45; Tom Glover, Scott Dirks, and Ward Gaines, *Blues with a Feeling: The Little Walter Story* (New York: Routledge, 2002), 99; Mitsutoshi Inaba, *Willie Dixon: Preacher of the Blues* (Lanham, Md.: Scarecrow Press, 2011), 325.

13. *Demings (N.Mex.) Headlight,* October 13, 1953; Jerry Osborne, *Rockin' Records Buyers-Sellers Reference Book and Price Guide, 2010 Edition* (Port Townsend, Wash.: Osborne Enterprises Publishing, 2010), 480; Discogs, "Chuck Higgins and His Mellotones," https://www.discogs.com/artist/3070223-Chuck-Higgins-His-Mellotones (accessed July 15, 2021); Mike Leadbitter, Neil Slaven, Leslie Fancourt, and Paul Maurice Pelletier, *Blues Records 1943–1970: A Selective Discography* (London, UK: Record Information Services, 1987), 555.

14. Ted Gioia, *West Coast Jazz: Modern Jazz in California, 1945–1960* (Berkeley: Univ. of California Press, 1992), 6–7. Sam Staggs, *Born to Be Hurt: The Untold Story of Imitation of Life* (New York: St. Martin's, 2009), 20–29. For a treatment of Eugene Jackson's career, including his work with Juanita Moore, see Eugene W. Jackson, Gwendolyn Sides St. Julian, *Eugene "Pineapple" Jackson: His Own Story* (Jefferson, N.C.: McFarland, 1999).

15. Sid Holt, ed., *The Rolling Stone Interviews: The 1980s* (New York: St. Martin's, 1989), 135.

16. Peter Guralnick, *Sam Phillips: The Man Who Invented Rock 'n' Roll* (New York: Little, Brown, 2015), 12–16; Sid Holt, ed., *The Rolling Stone Interviews: The 1980s*, 134.

17. Federal Writers' Project, *Tennessee: A Guide to the State, Complied and Written by the Federal Writers' Project of the Works Projects Administration for the State of Tennessee* (New York: Viking Press, 1939), 222; George W. Lee, *Beale Street: Where the Blues Began* (College Park, Md.: McGrath, 1934), v.

18. Henry Louis Gates Jr. and Cornell West, *The African-American Century: How Black Americans Have Shaped Our Country* (New York: Simon and Schuster, 2000), 58; Sebastian Danchin, *"Blues Boy": The Life and Music of B. B. King* (Jackson: Univ. Press of Mississippi, 1998), 20; Margaret McKee and Fred Chisenhall, *Beale Black and Blue: The Life and Music on America's Main Street* (Baton Rouge: Louisiana State Univ. Press, 1981), 127.

19. Louis Cantor, *Wheelin' on Beale: How WDIA-Memphis Became the Nation's First All-Black Radio Station and Created the Sound that Changed America* (New York: Pharos Books, 1992), 15–20; "WDIA, Sixth Memphis Station, Is Launched," *Broadcasting*, June 16, 1947, 79; William Barlow, *Voice Over: The Making of Black Radio* (Philadelphia: Temple Univ. Press, 1999), 121–125.

20. Earnestine Jenkins, "'The Voice of Memphis': WDIA, Nat D. Williams, and Black Radio Culture in the Early Civil Rights Era," *Tennessee Historical Quarterly* 65, no. 3 (fall 2006): 254–267; Craig Werner, *A Change Is Gonna Come: Music, Race and the Soul of America* (Ann Arbor: Univ. of Michigan Press, 2002), 74–75; Timothy Dodge, *Rhythm and Blues Goes Calypso* (Lanham, Md.: Lexington Books, 2019), 136.

21. *Pittsburgh (Pa.) Courier*, August 6, 1949; Earnestine Jenkins, "'The Voice of Memphis': WDIA, Nat D. Williams, and Black Radio Culture in the Early Civil Rights Era," 254–267; Louis Cantor, *Wheelin' on Beale: How WDIA-Memphis Became the Nation's First All-Black Radio Station and Created the Sound that Changed America*, 41–45.

22. *Pittsburgh (Pa.) Courier*, December 5, 1953; Louis Cantor, *Wheelin' on Beale: How WDIA-Memphis Became the Nation's First All-Black Radio Station and Created the Sound that Changed America*, 109–110; Thomas Hackett, "Rufus Thomas, the Man of Happiness," *Southern Cultures* 19, no. 1 (spring 2013): 112–116.

23. Craig Werner, *A Change Is Gonna Come: Music, Race and the Soul of America*, 75–76.

24. Becky Phillips, interview, "Sam Phillips: The Man Who Invented Rock and Roll," Sun Records—706 Union Avenue Sessions, http://www.706unionavenue.nl/64258532 (accessed October 21, 2021); Colin Escott with Martin Hawkins, *Good Rockin' Tonight: Sun Records and the Birth of Rock 'n' Roll* (New York: St. Martin's, 1991), 9–15; Peter Guralnick, *Sam Phillips: The Man Who Invented Rock 'n' Roll*, 40–52.

25. Sam Phillips, interview, "Sam Phillips: The Man Who Invented Rock and Roll," Sun

Records—706 Union Avenue Sessions, http://www.706unionavenue.nl/64258532 (accessed October 21, 2021); Sid Holt, ed., *The Rolling Stone Interviews: The 1980s*, 134; James A. Cosby, *Holy Rollers and Hillbillies: How America Gave Birth to Rock and Roll* (Jefferson, N.C.: McFarland, 2016), 124–126.

26. Colin Escott with Martin Hawkins, *Good Rockin' Tonight: Sun Records and the Birth of Rock 'n' Roll*, 14–40; Rick Kennedy and Randy McNutt, *Little Labels, Big Sound: Small Record Companies and the Rise of American Music* (Bloomington: Indiana Univ. Press, 1999), 92.

27. Charlie Gillett, "Rufus Thomas: Push and Pull That Funky Dog," *Record Mirror* (1971), https://www.rocksbackpages.com/Library/Article/rufus-thomas-push-and-pull-that-funky-dog (accessed November 5, 2021); Rufus Thomas, interview with Barney Hoskyns (1985), https://www.rocksbackpages.com/Library/Article/rufus-thomas-1985 (accessed October 10, 2021).

28. Charles L. Hughes, "'You Pay One Hell of a Price to Be Black': Rufus Thomas and the Racial Politics of Memphis Music," in *An Unseen Light: Black Struggles for Freedom in Memphis, Tennessee*, ed. Aram Goudsouzian and Charles W. McKinney Jr. (Lexington: Univ. Press of Kentucky, 2018), 228–253; David Fricke, "Rufus Thomas," *Rolling Stone*, January 31, 2002, 20; Rufus Thomas, interview with Charlie Gillett, *Record Mirror* (1971), https://www.rocksbackpages.com/Library/Article/rufus-thomas-push-and-pull-that-funky-dog (accessed October 10, 2021); Rufus Thomas, interview with Barney Hoskyns, https://www.rocksbackpages.com/Library/Article/rufus-thomas-1985 (accessed October 10, 2021).

29. Peter Guralnick, *Sam Phillips: The Man Who Invented Rock 'n' Roll*, 170.

30. Peter Guralnick, *Sam Phillips: The Man Who Invented Rock 'n' Roll*, 170–172; James L. Dickerson, *Goin' Back to Memphis: A Century of Blues, Rock 'n' Roll, and Glorious Soul* (New York: Schirmer Books, 1996), 90–91; Louis Cantor, *Wheelin' on Beale: How WDIA-Memphis Became the Nation's First All-Black Radio Station and Created the Sound that Changed America*, 94; Anthony DeCurtis, ed., and Robert Palmer, *Blues and Chaos: The Music Writing of Robert Palmer* (New York: Scribner, 2009), 129–130.

31. Peter Guralnick, *Sam Phillips: The Man Who Invented Rock 'n' Roll*, 171; *Billboard*, April 4, 1953, 28; Sun Records—706 Union Avenue Sessions, March 1, 1953–March 31, 1953, https://www.706unionavenue.nl/83574047 (accessed October 22, 2021).

32. *Billboard*, April 4, 1953; Sun Records—706 Union Avenue Sessions, March 1, 1953–March 31, 1953, https://www.706unionavenue.nl/83574047 (accessed October 22, 2021).

33. *Billboard*, March 28, 1953, April 4, 1953, April 11, 1953, April 18, 1953, April 25, 1953, May 2, 1953, May 9, 1953, May 16, 1953, May 23, 1953, May 30, 1953, June 6, 1953.

34. Sun Records—706 Union Avenue Sessions, March 1, 1953–March 31, 1953, http://www.706unionavenue.nl/64258532 (accessed October 21, 2021); *Billboard*, April 4, 1953; *Pittsburgh (Pa.) Courier*, August 8, 1953; *Knoxville (Tenn.) Journal*, May 3, 1953.

35. Sun Records—706 Union Avenue Sessions, March 1, 1953–March 31, 1953, http://www.706unionavenue.nl/64258532 (accessed October 21, 2021); *Knoxville (Tenn.) Journal*, May 3, 1953; *Jet*, June 4, 1953, 62.

36. *Billboard*, August 1, 1953; Larry Birnbaum, *Before Elvis: The Pre-History of Rock 'n' Roll*, 234; Brian Lukasavitz, "Blue Law: Hound Dog vs. Bear Cat," *American Blues Scene*, March

19, 2014, https://www.americanbluesscene.com/blues-law-hound-dog-vs-bear-cat/ (accessed November 5, 2021).

37. Larry Birnbaum, *Before Elvis: The Pre-History of Rock 'n' Roll,* 234; *Billboard,* April 4, 1953, April 11, 1953.

38. Anthony DeCurtis, ed., and Robert Palmer, *Blues and Chaos: The Music Writing of Robert Palmer* (New York: Scribner, 2009), 130.

39. Colin Escott with Martin Hawkins, *Good Rockin' Tonight: Sun Records and the Birth of Rock 'n' Roll,* 57; Sam Phillips interview, "Renegades," *Rock & Roll,* episode 1, documentary, directed by David Espar and Robert Levi (Boston, WBHG, London, BBC, 1995); Aram Goudsouzian and Charles W. McKinney Jr., eds., *An Unseen Light: Black Struggles for Freedom in Memphis, Tennessee,* 239; Charlie Gillett, "Rufus Thomas: Push and Pull That Funky Dog," *Record Mirror* (1971), https://www.rocksbackpages.com/Library/Article/rufus-thomas-push-and-pull-that-funky-dog (accessed November 5, 2021); *Billboard,* March 29, 1997.

40. *New York Times,* December 19, 2001.

Elvis

1. Glenn C. Altschuler, *All Shook Up: How Rock 'n' Roll Changed America* (New York: Oxford Univ. Press, 2003), 35.

2. The band was occasionally referred to as Freddie Bell and *His* Bellboys.

3. Jeremy Simmonds, *The Encyclopedia of Dead Rock Stars: Heroin, Handguns, and Ham Sandwiches* (Chicago: Chicago Review Press, 2006), 633; Michel Ruppli and Ed Novitsky, *The Mercury Label: The 1956 to 1964 Era* (Westport, Conn.: Greenwood Press, 1993), 37, 72, 635; Roberta Linn and Eric Meekss, *Not Now, Lord, I've Got Too Much to Do* (New York: iUniversal, 2005), 67; Cilin Larkin, *The Virgin Encyclopedia of Fifties Music* (London, UK: Virgin Books, 2002), 38; *Philadelphia Enquirer,* July 15, 1956; *Palm Springs (Calif.) Desert Sun,* February 17, 2008; *Chicago Tribune,* December 5, 1990.

4. Mike Weatherford, *Cult Vegas: The Weirdest! The Wildest! The Swingin'est Town on Earth!* (Las Vegas, Nev.: Huntington Press, 2001), 59; *Reno (Nev.) Gazette-Journal,* May 11, 1962; *Chester (Pa.) Delaware County Times,* December 22, 1954; *St. Louis Post-Dispatch,* October 24, 1954.

5. Ralph G. Giordano, *Pop Goes the Decade: The Fifties* (Westport, Conn.: Greenwood Press, 2017), 56–58; Lori Bindig, *Gossip Girl: A Critical Understanding* (Lanham, Md.: Lexington Books, 2015), 12–13; Don Rayno, *Paul Whiteman: Pioneer in American Music,* vol. 2, *1930–1967* (Lanham, Md.: Scarecrow Press, 2009), 278–280, 424; Sharon Marie Ross and Louisa Ellen Stein, eds., *Teen Television: Essays on Programming and Fandom* (Jefferson, N.C.: McFarland, 2008), 34–35; Jake Austen, *TV a-Go-Go: Rock on TV from American Bandstand to American Idol* (Chicago: Chicago Review Press, 2005), 27–28.

6. Larry Birnbaum, *Before Elvis: The Pre-History of Rock 'n' Roll,* 234–235; Mark Duffet, *Counting Down Elvis; His 100 Finest Songs* (New York: Rowman and Littlefield, 2018), 195–196; Josh Alan Friedman, *Tell the Truth Until They Bleed: Coming Clean in the Dirty World of Blues and Rock 'n' Roll,* 7–8; Ace Collins, *Untold Gold: The Story Behind Elvis's #1 Hits* (Chicago: Chicago Review Press, 2005), 29–30; Paul Zollo, *More Songwriters on Songwriting,* 38–39.

7. Spencer Leigh, *Elvis: Caught in a Trap* (Carmarthen, UK: McNidder and Grace, 2018), 157–158; Josh Alan Friedman, *Tell the Truth Until They Bleed: Coming Clean in the Dirty World of Blues and Rock 'n' Roll*, 7–8; Anne Dhu McLucas, *The Musical Ear: Oral Tradition in the USA* (Farnham, Surry, UK: Ashgate, 2010), 58; *Chester (Pa.) Delaware County Times*, December 22, 1954.

8. Jim Dawson, *Rock Around the Clock: The Record That Started a Revolution* (San Francisco: Backbeat Books, 2003), 148–149; Bill Haley Jr. and Peter Benjaminson, *Crazy Man, Crazy: The Bill Haley Story* (San Francisco: Backbeat Books, 2019), 86–88; *Las Vegas Review-Journal*, April 11, 1956; *Chicago Tribune*, December 5, 1990.

9. James P. Kraft, *Vegas at Odds: Labor Conflict in a Leisure Economy, 1960–1985* (Baltimore, Md.: Johns Hopkins Univ. Press, 2010), 71–73; *Las Vegas Review-Journal*, May 15, 1955.

10. George Klein and Chuck Crisafulli, *Elvis: My Best Man: Radio Days, Rock 'n' Roll Nights, and My Lifelong Friendship with Elvis Presley* (New York: Three Rivers Press, 2010), 16–17.

11. Peter Guralnick, *Last Train to Memphis: The Rise of Elvis Presley* (London, UK: Little, Brown, 1994), 68.

12. Michael T. Bertrand, *Race, Rock, and Elvis* (Chicago: Univ. of Illinois Press, 2000), 45–47; Benjamin Hooks, interview with Bruce Sinofsky et al. "When America Rocked," *10 Days that Unexpectedly Changed America* (New York: A&E Home Video, 2006).

13. Joel Williamson, *Elvis Presley: A Southern Life* (New York: Oxford Univ. Press, 2015), 145; Alanna Nash, *Baby, Let's Play House: Elvis Presley and the Women Who Loved Him* (New York: HarperCollins, 2010), 66; Albin J. Zak III, *I Don't Sound Like Nobody: Remaking Music in 1950s America* (Ann Arbor: Univ. of Michigan Press, 2012), 104; Ed Ward, *A History of Rock and Roll*, vol. 1 (New York: Flatiron Books, 2016), 77; *Philadelphia Daily News*, November 1, 1971; *Detroit Free Press*, October 3, 1977.

14. Scotty Moore, *Scotty and Elvis: Aboard the Mystery Train* (Jackson: Univ. Press of Mississippi, 1997), 48–52.

15. Peter Guralnick and Ernst Jorgensen, *Elvis Day by Day* (New York: Ballantine Books, 1999), 18; Sam Phillips interview, "Renegades," *Rock & Roll*, episode 1, documentary, directed by David Espar and Robert Levi (Boston, WBHG, London, BBC, 1995); Scotty Moore, *Scotty and Elvis: Aboard the Mystery Train*, 48–52.

16. Scotty Moore, *Scotty and Elvis: Aboard the Mystery Train*, 56; *Memphis (Tenn.) Commercial Appeal*, August 14, 2009; Louis Cantor, *Dewey and Elvis: The Life and Times of a Rock 'n' Roll Deejay* (Urbana, Ill.: Univ. of Chicago Press, 2005), 145; Jerry Schilling, *Me and a Guy Named Elvis: My Lifelong Friendship with Elvis Presley* (New York: Penguin Group, 2007), 10.

17. Louis Cantor, *Dewey and Elvis: The Life and Times of a Rock 'n' Roll Deejay*, 148–152; *San Angelo (Tex.) Standard-Times*, August 17, 1977; *Fort Worth (Tex.) Star-Telegram*, February 14, 1999; *Memphis (Tenn.) Commercial Appeal*, October 14, 1954; Scotty Moore interview, "Renegades," *Rock & Roll*, episode 1, documentary, directed by David Espar and Robert Levi (Boston, WBHG, London, BBC, 1995).

18. Tracey E. W. Laird, *Louisiana Hayride: Radio and Roots Along the Red River* (New York: Oxford Univ. Press, 2005), 10; Craig Morrison, *Go Cat Go!: Rockabilly Music and Its Makers* (Urbana: Univ. of Illinois Press, 1998), 3; Richard Aquila, *Let's Rock!: How 1950s America Cre-*

ated Elvis and the Rock and Roll Craze, 116–117; *Memphis (Tenn.) Commercial Appeal,* October 1, 6, 13, 14, 15, 1954; *Billboard,* August 7, 1954.

19. *Memphis (Tenn.) Commercial Appeal,* October 20, 1954.

20. Scotty Moore, *Scotty and Elvis: Aboard the Mystery Train,* 71–72; *Nashville (Tenn.) Tennessean,* December 22, 1955; *Boston Globe,* August 23, 1977; *Atlanta Constitution,* August 23, 1977; *Billboard,* May 23, 1970.

21. Alana Nash, *The Colonel: The Extraordinary Story of Colonel Tom Parker and Elvis Presley* (New York: Simon and Schuster, 2003), 12–13, 107–108; James L. Dickerson, *Colonel Tom Parker: The Curious Life of Elvis Presley's Eccentric Manager* (New York: Cooper Square Press, 2001, 2, 24; *Boston Globe,* March 25, 1984.

22. Ernst Jorgensen, *Elvis Presley: A Life in Music* (New York: St. Martin's, 1998), 28; Alana Nash, *The Colonel: The Extraordinary Story of Colonel Tom Parker and Elvis Presley,* 116–117.

23. Scotty Moore, *Scotty and Elvis: Aboard the Mystery Train,* 78; Horace Logan, *Elvis, Hank and Me: Making Musical History on the Louisiana Hayride* (New York: St. Martin's, 1998), 149.

24. Peter Guralnick, *Sam Phillips: The Man Who Invented Rock 'n' Roll,* 272; David Bruenger, *Making Money, Making Music: History and Core Concepts* (Oakland: Univ. of California Press, 2016), 118; Joel Williamson, *Elvis Presley: A Southern Life,* 39; Sam Phillips interview, "Renegades," *Rock & Roll,* episode 1, documentary, directed by David Espar and Robert Levi (Boston, WBHG, London, BBC, 1995); Colin Escott, *Good Rockin' Tonight: Sun Records and the Birth of Rock 'n' Roll,* 82.

25. *Nashville (Tenn.) Tennessean,* February 15, 1956; *Columbia (S.C.) Record,* April 26, 1956; *Billboard,* May 26, 1956; Alana Nash, *The Colonel: The Extraordinary Story of Colonel Tom Parker and Elvis Presley,* 135–136; Peter J. Levinson, *Tommy Dorsey: Livin' in a Great Big Way: A Biography* (Boston, Mass.: Da Capo, 2005), 289–291.

26. *Milton Berle Show,* National Broadcasting Company, original air date, April 3, 1956; *Los Angeles Times,* April 3, 1956; *New York Daily News,* April 3, 1956; Hank Bordowitz, *Turning Points in Rock and Roll* (New York: Kensington, 2004), 52.

27. *Chula Vista (Calif.) Star-News,* April 10, 1956; *Fort Lauderdale (Fla.) News,* April 10, 1956.

28. Richard Zoglin, *Elvis in Vegas: How the King Reinvented the Las Vegas Show* (New York: Simon and Schuster, 2019), 4–7; Richard Aquila, *Let's Rock!: How 1950s America Created Elvis and the Rock and Roll Craze,* 126–129; Peter Guralnick, *Last Train to Memphis: The Rise of Elvis Presley,* 270–272; Scotty Moore, *Scotty and Elvis: Aboard the Mystery Train,* 110–112; *Las Vegas Sun,* April 28, 1956; *Los Angeles Times,* April 24, 1956.

29. Richard Zoglin, *Elvis in Vegas: How the King Reinvented the Las Vegas Show,* 8; *Memphis Commercial Appeal,* May 6, 1956

30. *New York Daily News,* August 11, 1987.

31. Scotty Moore, *Scotty and Elvis: Aboard the Mystery Train,* 111.

32. *Chicago Tribune,* December 5, 1990; Mike Weatherford, *Cult Vegas: The Weirdest! The Wildest! The Swingin'est Town on Earth!,* 117–118; Peter Guralnick and Ernst Jorgensen, *Elvis Day by Day,* 72; Glen Jeansonne, David Luhrssen, and Dan Sokolovic, *Elvis Presley, Reluctant Rebel: His Life and Times* (Santa Barbara, Calif.: Praeger, 2011) 122; D. J. Fontana and Scotty

Moore, interview with Arjan Deelen, http://elvisnews.dk/scotty-moore-and-dj-fontana-interview/ (accessed March 28, 2021).

33. Michael Spörke, *Big Mama Thornton: The Life and Music,* 106, 134.

34. *Jet,* August 1, 1957, August 31, 1987; Don Rhodes, *Say It Loud!: The Life of James Brown, Soul Brother No. 1* (Guilford, Conn.: Globe Pequot Press, 2009), 67–69; Neal Gregory and Janice Gregory, *When Elvis Died: Media Overload and the Origins of the Elvis Cult* (New York: Pharos Books, 1980), 109; Eric Charry, *A New and Concise History of Rock and R&B Through the Early 1990s* (Middletown, Conn.: Wesleyan Univ. Press, 2020). 56–57; Louis Cantor, *Wheelin' on Beale: How WDIA-Memphis Became the Nation's First All-Black Radio Station and Created the Sound that Changed America,* 189–196.

35. *Jet,* August 31, 1987.

36. *Des Moines (Iowa) Register,* May 23, 1956;

37. Peter Guralnick and Ernst Jorgensen, *Elvis Day by Day,* 73; Trevor Cajiao et al., *Shock, Rattle and Roll: Elvis Photographed During the Milton Berle Show* (New York: Sterling, 1998), 8–14; Ralph J. Gleason, "Dawn of True Sexual Hysteria," *Rolling Stone,* February 1, 1969, 20; *Oakland Tribune,* June 1, 1956, June 4, 1956, June 5, 1956.

38. Trevor Cajiao et al., *Shock, Rattle and Roll: Elvis Photographed During the Milton Berle Show,* 8–14.

39. Tracey E. W. Laird, *Louisiana Hayride: Radio and Roots Along the Red River,* 139; Ken Burke and Dan Griffin, *The Blue Moon Boys: The Story of Elvis Presley's Band* (Chicago: Chicago Review Press, 2006), 52; D. J. Fontana interview, https://www.youtube.com/watch?v=RAIYHXG8TVg (accessed March 1, 2021); D. J. Fontana, interview with Arjan Deelen, Elvis Australia, https://www.elvis.com.au/presley/interview-djfontana.shtml (accessed March 9, 2021).

40. *Ventura (Calif.) County Star-Free Press,* June 7, 1956; Leonard Bennett, "Who the Hell Is Elvis Presley?," *Cabaret,* August, 1956, 22; D. J. Fontana interview, "Renegades," *Rock & Roll,* episode 1, documentary, directed by David Espar and Robert Levi (Boston, WBHG, London, BBC, 1995).

41. *Milton Berle Show,* National Broadcasting Company (NBC), original air date June 5, 1956.

42. *New York Times,* June 6, 1956; *New York Daily News,* June 8, 1956; *Santa Rosa (Calif.) Press Democrat,* June 10, 1956; *San Francisco Examiner,* August 16, 1977.

43. Jerry Osborne, *Elvis, Word for Word: What He Said, Exactly How He Said It . . .* (New York: Gramercy, 2006), 40–41.

44. *New York Daily News,* July 2, 1956.

45. *Detroit Free Press,* June 16, 1956; *Los Angeles Times,* June 16, 1956; *St. Louis Globe-Democrat,* June 22, 1956; *Oakland (Calif.) Tribune,* June 21, 1956.

46. *Charlotte (N.C.) News,* June 28, 1956.

47. *Detroit Free Press,* June 28, 1956; *U.S. News and World Report,* March 13, 1978.

48. Steve Allen, *Hi-Ho Steverino!: My Adventures in the Wonderful, Wacky World of TV* (Fort Lee, N.J.: Barricade Books, 1994), 171–173; *Charlotte (N.C.) News,* June 28, 1956.

49. Scotty Moore, *Scotty and Elvis: Aboard the Mystery Train,* 112; Alana Nash, *The Colonel: The Extraordinary Story of Colonel Tom Parker and Elvis Presley,* 234–235.

50. *Steve Allen Show,* National Broadcasting Company, original air date, July 1, 1956; *Boston Globe,* July 2, 1956.

51. *Steve Allen Show,* National Broadcasting Company, original air date, July 1, 1956; Steve Allen, *Mark It and Strike It: An Autobiography* (New York: Holt, Rinehart and Winston, 1960), 185; David Inman, *Television Variety Shows: Histories and Episode Guides to 57 Programs* (Jefferson, N.C.: McFarland, 2006), 9; *Los Angeles Times,* June 30, 1956.

52. Steve Allen, *Hi-Ho Steverino!: My Adventures in the Wonderful, Wacky World of TV,* 172.

53. Elvis Presley interview, *Hy Gardner Calling,* New York, WRCA-TV, original air date July 1, 1956.

54. *Fort Worth (Tex.) Star-Telegram,* July 2, 1956; *Boston Globe,* July 2, 1956; *New York Daily News,* July 2, 1950; *Los Angeles Times,* July 3, 1956; *Newsweek,* July 3, 1956.

55. *Boston Globe,* July 2, 1956; *New York Daily News,* July 2, 1950; *Los Angeles Times,* July 3, 1956.

56. New York *Daily News,* September 11, 1956.

57. Alfred Wertheimer, *Elvis '56: In the Beginning* (New York: Macmillan, 1979), 78–79.

58. Alfred Wertheimer, *Elvis '56: In the Beginning,* 78–80; Peter Guralnick, *Last Train to Memphis: The Rise of Elvis Presley,* 297–299; Patrick Humphries, *Elvis, the #1 Hits: A Secret History of the Classics* (Kansas City: Andrew McMeel Publishing, 2003). 26; Scotty Moore, *Scotty and Elvis: Aboard the Mystery Train,* 113.

59. Alfred Wertheimer, *Elvis '56: In the Beginning,* 78–80; Scotty Moore, *Scotty and Elvis: Aboard the Mystery Train,* 113–114.

60. *Billboard,* July 21, 1956.

61. *Memphis Commercial Appeal.* July 5, 1956.

62. *Baltimore Sun,* August 5, 1956; *New York Daily News,* September 16, 1956; *Cashbox,* July 28, 1956.

63. *Indianapolis (Ind.) News,* August 2, 1956; *Saturday Evening Post,* January 1, 1960; Richard Zoglin, *Elvis in Vegas: How the King Reinvented the Las Vegas Show,* 78; Larry Birnbaum, *Before Elvis: The Prehistory of Rock 'n' Roll,* 22; Brian Ward, *Just My Soul Responding: Rhythm and Blues, Black Consciousness, and Race Relations* (London, UK: UCL Press, 1998), 117–118; Peter Guralnick, *Last Train to Memphis: The Rise of Elvis Presley,* 384.

64. Jerry Leiber and Mike Stoller, *Late Night with David Letterman,* National Broadcasting Company (NBC), original air date March 27, 1987; *Chicago Tribune,* July 21, 1956.

65. Jerry Leiber and Mike Stoller, with David Ritz, *Hound Dog: The Leiber and Stoller Autobiography,* 93–95.

66. Jerry Leiber and Mike Stoller, with David Ritz, *Hound Dog: The Leiber and Stoller Autobiography,* 86–88.

67. Jerry Leiber and Mike Stoller, with David Ritz, *Hound Dog: The Leiber and Stoller Autobiography,* 86–88; Jerry Leiber and Mike Stoller, *Late Night with David Letterman,* National Broadcasting Company (NBC), original air date March 27, 1987.

68. James Maguire, *Impresario: The Life and Times of Ed Sullivan* (New York: Billboard Books, 2006), 190–192; Bernie Ilson, *Sundays with Sullivan: How* The Ed Sullivan Show *Brought Elvis, the Beatles, and Culture to America* (Lanham, Md.: Rowman and Littlefield,

2009), 53–54; *New York Daily News,* September 16, 1956; *Memphis (Tenn.) Press-Scimitar,* October 10, 1956; *Los Angeles Times,* September 12, 1956.

69. *Binghamton (N.Y.) Press and Sun-Bulletin,* September 5, 1956; *North Hollywood (Calif.) Valley Times,* September 7, 1956; *Des Moines (Iowa) Register,* September 9, 1956.

70. *Ed Sullivan Show,* Columbia Broadcasting System (CBS), original air date September 9, 1956; *Philadelphia Inquirer,* September 10, 1956.

71. *Ed Sullivan Show,* Columbia Broadcasting System (CBS), original air date September 9, 1956.

72. *Hempstead (N.Y.) Newsday,* September 10, 1956; *New York Daily News,* September 11, 1956.

73. *Ed Sullivan Show,* Columbia Broadcasting System (CBS), original air date October 28, 1956; *New York Daily News,* October 30, 1956.

74. *Ed Sullivan Show,* Columbia Broadcasting System (CBS), original air date October 28, 1956; *Los Angeles Mirror,* November 1, 1956.

75. *Ed Sullivan Show,* Columbia Broadcasting System (CBS), original air date January 6, 1957.

76. *Ed Sullivan Show,* Columbia Broadcasting System (CBS), original air date January 6, 1957.

77. *San Francisco Examiner,* October 28, 1956; *Arizona Daily Star* (Tucson, Ariz.), November 2, 1956.

Epilogue

1. *Rolling Stone,* Rolling Stone 500 Greatest Songs of All Time, vol. 1, 1950s–1960s (Van Nuys, Calif.: Alfred, 2008), 11.

Bibliography

PRIMARY SOURCES

Collections

Middle Tennessee State University, Murfreesboro, Tennessee. The Center for Popular Music. Don Robey Collection.

Rock and Roll Hall of Fame Archives, Cleveland, Ohio. Collection on Elvis Presley.

Rock and Roll Hall of Fame Archives, Cleveland, Ohio. Scotty Moore Papers.

University of Memphis, Memphis, Tennessee. McWherter Library, Special Collections.

Published Primary Sources

Allen, Steve. *Hi-Ho Steverino!: My Adventures in the Wonderful, Wacky World of TV.* Fort Lee, N.J.: Barricade Books, 1994.

———. *Mark It and Strike It: An Autobiography.* New York: Holt, Rinehart and Winston, 1960.

Federal Writers' Project. *Tennessee: A Guide to the State, Complied and Written by the Federal Writers' Project of the Works Projects Administration for the State of Tennessee.* New York: Viking Press, 1939.

Fricke, David. "Leiber and Stoller: Rolling Stone's 1990 Interview with the Songwriting Legends." *Rolling Stone,* August 22, 2011.

Gaines, Grady, with Rod Evans. *I've Been Out There: On the Road with Legends of Rock 'n' Roll.* College Station: Texas A&M Univ. Press, 2015.

Greensmith, Bill, Mike Rowe, and Mark Camarigg, eds. *Blues Unlimited: Essential Interviews from the Original Blues Magazine.* Chicago: Univ. of Illinois Press, 2015.

Holt, Sid, ed. *The Rolling Stone Interviews: The 1980s* (New York: St. Martin's, 1989).

Jackson, Eugene W., and Gwendolyn Sides St. Julian. *Eugene "Pineapple" Jackson: His Own Story.* Jefferson, N.C.: McFarland, 1999.

Klein, George, and Chuck Crisafulli, *Elvis: My Best Man: Radio Days, Rock 'n' Roll Nights, and My Lifelong Friendship with Elvis Presley.* New York: Three Rivers Press, 2010.

Leiber, Jerry, and Mike Stoller, with David Ritz. *Hound Dog: The Leiber and Stoller Autobiography.* New York: Simon and Schuster, 2009.

Linn, Roberta, and Eric Meekss. *Not Now, Lord, I've Got Too Much to Do.* New York: iUniversal, 2005.

Love, Preston. *A Thousand Honey Creeks Later: My Life in Music, from Basie to Motown—and Beyond.* Middletown, Conn.: Wesleyan Univ. Press, 1997.

Moore, Scotty. *Scotty and Elvis: Aboard the Mystery Train.* Jackson: Univ. Press of Mississippi, 1997.

Myers, Mark. *Anatomy of a Song: The Oral History of 45 Iconic Hits That Changed Rock, R&B and Pop.* New York: Grove Press, 2016.

Osborne, Jerry. *Elvis, Word for Word: What He Said, Exactly How He Said It . . .* New York: Gramercy, 2006.

Otis, Johnny. *Listen to the Lambs.* New York: Norton, 1968.

———. *Upside Your Head: Rhythm and Blues on Central Avenue.* Hanover, N.H.: Univ. Press of New England, 1993.

Polk, R. L., and Company, *Baltimore City Directory, 1930* (Detroit, Mich.: R. L. Polk, 1930).

Schilling, Jerry. *Me and a Guy Named Elvis: My Lifelong Friendship with Elvis Presley.* New York: Penguin Group, 2007.

Thomas, Rufus. Interview with Charlie Gillett, *Record Mirror* (1971). Rocksbackpages.com.

———. Interview with Barney Hoskyns (1985). Rocksbackpages.com.

White, Charles. *The Life and Times of Little Richard: The Authorized Biography.* London, UK: Omnibus Press, 1984.

Zollo, Paul. *More Songwriters on Songwriting.* Boston, Mass.: Da Capo, 2016.

Electronic Media Interviews

Boggs, Bill, Jerry Leiber, and Mike Stoller. *Jerry Leiber and Mike Stoller Full Interview with Bill Boggs.* BillBoggsTV.

Fontana, D. J. Interview. https://www.youtube.com/watch?v=RAIYHXG8TVg. Accessed March 1, 2021.

———. Interview. "Renegades." *Rock & Roll.* Documentary, episode 1, directed by Davis Espar and Robert Levi. Boston, WBHG; London, BBC, 1995.

Fontana, D. J., and Scotty Moore. Interview with Arjan Deelen. http://elvisnews.dk/scotty-moore-and-dj-fontana-interview/. Accessed March 28, 2021.

Gillett, Charlie, and Johnny Otis. *Interview with Johnny Otis* (1970). Rocksbackpages.com.

Gross, Terry, and Johnny Otis. *Fresh Air with Terry Gross: Interview with Johnny Otis.* National Public Radio, WHYY Public Media, Philadelphia, Pennsylvania. Original air date November 21, 1989.

Hooks, Benjamin. Interview with Bruce Sinofsky et al. "When America Rocked." *10 Days that Unexpectedly Changed America.* New York: A&E Home Video, 2006.

Leiber, Jerry, and Mike Stoller. *Late Night With David Letterman,* National Broadcasting Company (NBC). Original air date March 27, 1987.

Leslie, Paul, and Mike Stoller. Interview with Mike Stoller. *The Paul Leslie Hour.*

Moore, Scotty. Interview. "Renegades." *Rock & Roll.* Episode 1, documentary, directed by David Espar and Robert Levi. Boston, WBHG, London, BBC, 1995.

Otis, Johnny. "Rock and Roll Hall of Fame Induction Speech, 1994." Rock and Roll Hall of Fame, Cleveland, Ohio.

Phillips, Becky. Interview. "Sam Phillips: The Man Who Invented Rock and Roll." Sun Records—706 Union Avenue Sessions. http://www.706unionavenue.nl/64258532

Phillips, Sam. Interview. "Renegades." *Rock & Roll.* Episode 1, documentary, directed by Davis Espar and Robert Levi. Boston, WBHG; London, BBC, 1995.

Presley, Elvis. Interview. *Hy Gardner Calling.* New York: WRCA-TV. Original air date July 1, 1956.

"Rock and Roll; In The Groove; *Interview with Jerry Leiber and Mike Stoller* [Part 1 of 7]." WGBH Media Library and Archives. http://openvault.wgbh.org/catalog/V_3B7201E645E8476797EB49ECC8B901C1.

Roeser, Steve, and Johnny Otis. "Interview with Johnny Otis" (1990). Rocksbackpages.com.

Springsteen, Bruce. *Desert Island Discs.* British Broadcasting Company (BBC) Radio, 2016.

Strachwitz, Chris, and Willie Mae Thornton. *Big Mama Thornton Interview* (date unknown). The Chris Strachwitz Collection, Arhoolie Foundation.

Smith, Joe, and Jerry Leiber. *Off the Record Interview with Jerry Leiber, (1988?).* Audio recording. Library of Congress, Washington, D.C.

Smith, Joe, and Lester Sill. *Off the Record Interview with Lester Sill, 1986-03-13.* Audio recording. Library of Congress, Washington, D.C.

Network Television Programs

Ed Sullivan Show. Columbia Broadcasting System (CBS). Original air date September 9, 1956.

Ed Sullivan Show. Columbia Broadcasting System (CBS). Original air date October 28, 1956.

Ed Sullivan Show. Columbia Broadcasting System (CBS). Original air date January 6, 1957.

Late Night With David Letterman. National Broadcasting Company (NBC). Original air date March 27, 1987.

Milton Berle Show. National Broadcasting Company (NBC). Original air date, April 3, 1956.

Milton Berle Show. National Broadcasting Company (NBC). Original air date, June 5, 1956.

Steve Allen Show. National Broadcasting Company (NBC). Original air date, July 1, 1956.

Government Documents

California Department of Health Services. *California Birth Index, 1905–1995,* California Department of Health Services, Center for Health Statistics, Sacramento, California.

California Department of Public Health. County Birth, Marriage, and Death Records, 1830–1980.

Harris County, Texas. Marriage Records. Harris County Clerk's Office, Houston, Texas.

Library of Congress. *Catalogue of Copyright Entries: Unpublished Music, Jan.–June, 1952,* third series, vol. 6, part 5b, N. 1. Washington, D.C.: Library of Congress, 1953.

United States, *World War I Draft Registration Cards, 1917–1918* (on-line database). Ancestry.com.

United States. *WWII Draft Cards, Young Men, 1940–1947* (on-line database). Ances try.com.

United States Census, 1910, Bronx Assembly District 32. New York, New York.

United States Census, 1920, Alameda, Oakland, California.

United States Census, 1930, Alameda, Berkeley, California.

United States Census, 1940, Alameda, Oakland, California.

United States Census. 1940. Baltimore, Baltimore City, Maryland.

United States Census. 1940. New York, Queens, New York.

United States District Court S.D. New York. *Valjo Music Publishing Corporation, Plaintiff v. Elvis Presley Music, Inc., Mike Stoller and Jerry Leiber, Defendants.* December 4, 1957.

United States Social Security Administration. *Social Security Death Index, Master File.* United States Social Security Administration, Washington D.C.

Newspapers and Magazines

Anniston (Ala.) Star
Altoona (Pa.) Tribune
Atlanta Constitution
Baltimore (Md.) Sun
Billboard
Binghamton (N.Y.) Press and Sun-Bulletin
Boston Globe
Broadcasting
Brooklyn (N.Y.) Eagle
Caberet
Cashbox
Charlotte (N.C.) News
Charlotte (N.C.) Observer
Chester (Pa.) Delaware County Times
Chula Vista (Calif.) Star-News
Chicago Tribune
Columbia (S.C.) Record
Demings (N.Mex.) Headlight
Des Moines (Iowa) Register
Detroit Free Press
El Paso (Tex.) Times
Fort Lauderdale (Fla.) News
Fort Worth (Tex.) Star-Telegram
Franklin (Ind.) Evening Star
Freehold (N.J.) Transcript and Monmouth Inquirer
Hagerstown (Md.) Morning Call
Hempstead (N.Y.) Newsday
Honolulu (Hawaii) Star-Bulletin
Houston Chronicle

Indianapolis (Ind.) News
Ithaca (N.Y.) Journal
Jet
Knoxville (Tenn.) Journal
Las Vegas Review-Journal
Las Vegas Sun
Living Blues
Los Angeles Mirror
Los Angeles Times
Memphis (Tenn.) Commercial Appeal
Memphis (Tenn.) Press-Scimitar
Miami (Fla.) News
Muncie (Ind.) Star Press
Nashville (Tenn.) Banner
Nashville (Tenn.) Tennessean
New Musical Express
New York Age
New York Daily News
New York Times
Newsweek
North Hollywood (Calif.) Valley Times
Oakland Tribune
Oklahoma City (Okla.) Daily Oklahoman
Palm Springs (Calif.) Desert Sun
Pasadena (Calif.) Independent
Philadelphia Daily News
Philadelphia Enquirer
Pittsburgh (Pa.) Courier
Reno (Nev.) Gazette-Journal
Rolling Stone
Roseville (Calif.) Press-Tribune
Saint George (Utah) Daily Spectrum
St. Louis Globe-Democrat
St. Louis Post-Dispatch
San Angelo (Tex.) Standard-Times
San Francisco Examiner
Santa Rosa (Calif.) Press Democrat
Saturday Evening Post

Topanga (Calif.) Journal
Arizona Daily Star (Tucson, Arizona)
Ventura (Calif.) County Star-Free Press
U.S. News and World Report
Wall Street Journal
Washington Post

SECONDARY SOURCES

Books and Articles

Altschuler, Glenn C. *All Shook Up: How Rock 'n' Roll Changed America.* New York: Oxford Univ. Press, 2003.

Aparicio, Frances R., and Candida F. Jaquez, eds. *Musical Migrations: Transnationalism and Cultural Hybridity in Latino America,* vol. 1. New York: Palgrave Macmillan, 2003.

Aquila, Richard. *Let's Rock: How 1950s America Created Elvis and the Rock and Roll Craze.* New York: Rowman and Littlefield, 2017.

Austen, Jake. *TV a-Go-Go: Rock on TV from American Bandstand to American Idol.* Chicago: Chicago Review Press, 2005.

Banfield, William C. *Black Notes: Essays of a Musician Writing in the Post-Album Age.* Lanham, Md.: Scarecrow Press, 2004.

Barlow, William. *Voice Over: The Making of Black Radio.* Philadelphia: Temple Univ. Press, 1999.

Behnken, Brian D. *The Struggle in Black and Brown: African American and Mexican American Relations During the Civil Rights Era.* Lincoln: Univ. of Nebraska Press, 2011.

Bertrand, Michael T. *Race, Rock, and Elvis.* Chicago: Univ. of Illinois Press, 2000.

Bindig, Lori. *Gossip Girl: A Critical Understanding.* Lanham, Md.: Lexington Books, 2015.

Birnbaum, Larry. *Before Elvis: The Pre-History of Rock 'n' Roll.* Lanham, Md.: Scarecrow Press, 2013.

Bordowitz, Hank. *Dirty Little Secrets of the Record Business.* Chicago: Chicago Review Press, 2007.

Bordowitz, Hank. *Turning Points in Rock and Roll.* New York: Kensington, 2004.

Broven, John. *Record Makers and Breakers: Voices of Independent Rock 'n' Roll Pioneers.* Champaign: Univ. of Illinois Press, 2009.

Bruenger, David. *Making Money, Making Music: History and Core Concepts.* Oakland: Univ. of California Press, 2016.

Burke, David. "Big Mama Thornton: Big Mama's Blues." *Vintage Rock* (2017). Rocksbackpages.com.

Burke, Ken, and Dan Griffin. *The Blue Moon Boys: The Story of Elvis Presley's Band.* Chicago: Chicago Review Press, 2006.

Cajiao, Trevor, et al., *Shock, Rattle and Roll: Elvis Photographed During the Milton Berle Show.* New York: Sterling, 1998.

Campbell, Michael. *Popular Music in America: The Beat Goes On,* 4th ed. Boston, Mass.: Schirmer Cengage Learning, 2013.

Cantor, Louis. *Dewey and Elvis: The Life and Times of a Rock 'n' Roll Deejay.* Urbana, Ill.: Univ. of Chicago Press, 2005.

———. *Wheelin' on Beale: How WDIA-Memphis Became the Nation's First All-Black Radio Station and Created the Sound that Changed America.* New York: Pharos Books, 1992.

Cateforis, Theo, ed. *The Rock History Reader.* New York: Routledge, 2007.

Charry, Eric. *A New and Concise History of Rock and R&B Through the Early 1990s.* Middletown, Conn.: Wesleyan Univ. Press, 2020.

Collins, Ace. *Untold Gold: The Story Behind Elvis's #1 Hits.* Chicago: Chicago Review Press, 2005.

Cosby, James A. *Holy Rollers and Hillbillies: How America Gave Birth to Rock and Roll.* Jefferson, N.C.: McFarland, 2016.

Danchin, Sebastian. *"Blues Boy": The Life and Music of B. B. King.* Jackson: Univ. Press of Mississippi, 1998.

Dawson, Jim. *Rock Around the Clock: The Record That Started a Revolution.* San Francisco: Backbeat Books, 2003.

DeCurtis, Anthony, ed., and Robert Palmer. *Blues and Chaos: The Music Writing of Robert Palmer.* New York: Scribner, 2009.

Dickerson, James L. *Colonel Tom Parker: The Curious Life of Elvis Presley's Eccentric Manager.* New York: Cooper Square Press, 2001.

———. *Goin' Back to Memphis: A Century of Blues, Rock 'n' Roll, and Glorious Soul.* New York: Schirmer Books, 1996.

Dodge, Timothy. *Rhythm and Blues Goes Calypso.* Lanham, Md.: Lexington Books, 2019.

Driggs, Frank, and Chuck Haddix. *Kansas City Jazz: From Ragtime to Bebop—A History.* New York: Oxford Univ. Press, 2005.

Duffet, Mark. *Counting Down Elvis: His 100 Finest Songs.* New York: Rowman and Littlefield, 2018.

Eagle, Robert L., and Eric S. LeBlanc. *Blues: A Regional Experience.* Santa Barbara, Calif.: Praeger, 2013.

Emerson, Ken. *Always Magic in the Air: The Bomp and Brilliance of the Brill Building Era.* London: Fourth Estate, 2006.

Erlewine, Michael, Vladimir Bogdanov, Chris Woodstra, and Stephen Thomas Erlewine, eds. *All Music Guide to Country: The Experts' Guide to the Best Recordings in Country Music.* San Francisco: Miller Freeman Books, 1995.

Escott, Colin, with Martin Hawkins. *Good Rockin' Tonight: Sun Records and the Birth of Rock 'n' Roll.* New York: St. Martin's, 1991.

Farley, Charles. *Soul of the Man: Bobby "Blue" Bland.* Jackson: Univ. Press of Mississippi, 2011.

Fox, John Hartley. *King of the Queen City: The Story of King Records.* Champaign: Univ. of Illinois Press, 2009.

Fricke, David. "Rufus Thomas." *Rolling Stone,* January 31, 2002.

Friedman, Josh Alan. *Tell the Truth Until They Bleed: Coming Clean in the Dirty World of Blues and Rock 'n' Roll.* Milwaukee, Wisc.: Backbeat Books, 2008.

Gart, Galen, ed. *First Pressings: A History of Rhythm and Blues,* vol. 3. Charlottesville: Univ. of Virginia Press, 1986.

Gates, Henry Louis, Jr., and Cornell West. *The African-American Century: How Black Americans Have Shaped Our Country.* New York: Simon and Schuster, 2000.

George, Nelson. *The Death of Rhythm & Blues.* New York: Penguin, 1988.

Gioia, Ted. *West Coast Jazz: Modern Jazz in California, 1945–1960.* Berkeley: Univ. of California Press, 1992.

Giordano, Ralph G. *Pop Goes the Decade: The Fifties.* Westport, Conn.: Greenwood Press, 2017.

Gleason, Ralph J. "Dawn of True Sexual Hysteria." *Rolling Stone,* February 1, 1969.

Glover, Tom, Scott Dirks, and Ward Gaines. *Blues with a Feeling: The Little Walter Story.* New York: Routledge, 2002.

Goudsouzian, Aram, and Charles W. McKinney Jr., eds. *An Unseen Light: Black Struggles for Freedom in Memphis, Tennessee.* Lexington: Univ. Press of Kentucky, 2018.

Gregory, Neal, and Janice Gregory, *When Elvis Died: Media Overload and the Origins of the Elvis Cult.* New York: Pharos Books, 1980.

Griffiths, David. *Hot Jazz: From Harlem to Storyville.* Lanham, Md.: Scarecrow Press, 1998.

Guralnick, Peter. *Last Train to Memphis: The Rise of Elvis Presley.* London, UK: Little, Brown, 1994.

———. *Sam Phillips: The Man Who Invented Rock 'n' Roll.* New York: Little, Brown, 2015.

Guralnick, Peter, and Ernst Jorgensen. *Elvis Day by Day.* New York: Ballantine Books, 1999.

Hackett, Thomas. "Rufus Thomas, the Man of Happiness." *Southern Cultures* 19, no. 1 (spring 2013): 112–116.

Haley, Bill, Jr., and Peter Benjaminson. *Crazy Man, Crazy: The Bill Haley Story.* San Francisco: Backbeat Books, 2019.

Hoffman, Frank. ed. *Encyclopedia of Recorded Sound,* vol. 1. New York: Routledge, 2005.

Hoskyns, Barney. *Waiting for the Sun: A Rock 'n' Roll History of Los Angeles.* Milwaukee, Wisc.: Backbeat Books, 1996.

Hughes, Charles L. "'You Pay One Hell of a Price to Be Black': Rufus Thomas and the Racial Politics of Memphis Music." In *An Unseen Light: Black Struggles for Freedom in Memphis, Tennessee,* edited by Aram Goudsouzian and Charles W. McKinney Jr., 228–253. Lexington: Univ. Press of Kentucky, 2018.

Humphries, Patrick. *Elvis, the #1 Hits: A Secret History of the Classics.* Kansas City: Andrew McMeel Publishing, 2003.

Hurd, Jud. *Cartoon Success Secrets: A Tribute to 35 Years of Cartoonist Profiles.* Kansas City, Mo.: Andrews McMeel Publishing, 2004.

Ilson, Bernie. *Sundays with Sullivan: How* The Ed Sullivan Show *Brought Elvis, the Beatles, and Culture to America.* Lanham, Md.: Rowman and Littlefield, 2009.

Inaba, Mitsutoshi. *Willie Dixon: Preacher of the Blues.* Lanham, Md.: Scarecrow Press, 2011.

Inman, David. *Television Variety Shows: Histories and Episode Guides to 57 Programs.* Jefferson, N.C.: McFarland, 2006.

Jeansonne, Glen, David Luhrssen, and Dan Sokolovic. *Elvis Presley, Reluctant Rebel: His Life and Times.* Santa Barbara, Calif.: Praeger, 2011.

Jenkins, Earnestine. "'The Voice of Memphis': WDIA, Nat D. Williams, and Black Radio Culture in the Early Civil Rights Era." *Tennessee Historical Quarterly* 65, no. 3 (fall 2006): 254–267.

Jorgensen, Ernst. *Elvis Presley: A Life in Music.* New York: St. Martin's, 1998.

Kaplan, James. *Sinatra: The Chairman.* New York: Anchor, 2016.

Kennedy, Rick, and Randy McNutt. *Little Labels, Big Sound: Small Record Companies and the Rise of American Music.* Bloomington: Indiana Univ. Press, 1999.

Kirchner, Bill. ed. *The Oxford Companion to Jazz.* New York: Oxford Univ. Press, 2000.

Komara, Edward, and Peter Lee, eds. *The Blues Encyclopedia.* New York: Routledge, 2004.

Kraft, James P. *Vegas at Odds: Labor Conflict in a Leisure Economy, 1960–1985.* Baltimore, Md.: Johns Hopkins Univ. Press, 2010.

Laird, Tracey E. W. *Louisiana Hayride: Radio and Roots Along the Red River.* New York: Oxford Univ. Press, 2005.

Larkin, Cilin. *The Virgin Encyclopedia of Fifties Music.* London, UK: Virgin Books, 2002.

Lauterbach, Preston. "Sympathy for the Devil." *Oxford American* 87 (winter 2014).

Leadbitter, Mike, Neil Slaven, Leslie Fancourt, and Paul Maurice Pelletier. *Blues Records 1943–1970: A Selective Discography.* London, UK: Record Information Services, 1987.

Lee, George W. *Beale Street: Where the Blues Began.* College Park, Md.: McGrath, 1934.

Leigh, Spencer. *Elvis: Caught in a Trap.* Carmarthen, UK: McNidder and Grace, 2018.

Leszczak, Bob. *Who Did It First?: Great Rhythm and Blues Cover Songs and Their Original Artists.* Langham, Md.: Scarecrow Press, 2013.

Levinson, Peter J. *Tommy Dorsey: Livin' in a Great Big Way: A Biography.* Boston, Mass.: Da Capo, 2005.

Lipsitz, George. *Midnight at the Barrelhouse: The Johnny Otis Story.* Minneapolis: Univ. of Minnesota Press, 2010.

———. *Time Passages: Collective Memory and American Popular Culture.* Minneapolis: Univ. of Minnesota Press, 1990.

Logan, Horace. *Elvis, Hank and Me: Making Musical History on the Louisiana Hayride.* New York: St. Martin's, 1998.

Lukasavitz, Brian. "Blue Law: Hound Dog vs. Bear Cat." *American Blues Scene,* March 19, 2014. https://www.americanbluesscene.com/blues-law-hound-dog-vs-bear-cat/.

Lydon, Michael. *Ray Charles: Man and Music.* New York: Routledge, 2004.

McGee, David. *B.B. King: There Is Always One More Time.* San Francisco: Backbeat Books, 2005.

Maguire, James. *Impresario: The Life and Times of Ed Sullivan.* New York: Billboard Books, 2006.

McKee, Margaret, and Fred Chisenhall. *Beale Black and Blue: The Life and Music on America's Main Street* (Baton Rouge: Louisiana State Univ. Press, 1981).

McLucas, Anne Dhu. *The Musical Ear: Oral Tradition in the USA.* Farnham, Surry, UK: Ashgate, 2010.

Millar, Bill. "Leiber and Stoller Part One: The Blues (1950–1953)." *Let It Rock* (1974). Rocksbackpages.com.

Morrison, Craig. *Go Cat Go!: Rockabilly Music and Its Makers.* Urbana: Univ. of Illinois Press, 1998.

Nash, Alanna. *Baby, Let's Play House: Elvis Presley and the Women Who Loved Him.* New York: HarperCollins, 2010.

Nash, Alana. *The Colonel: The Extraordinary Story of Colonel Tom Parker and Elvis Presley.* New York: Simon and Schuster, 2003.

O'Brien, Timothy J., and David Ensminger. *Mojo Hand: The Life and Music of Lightnin' Hopkins.* Austin: Univ. of Texas Press, 2013.

O'Connell, Sean J. *Images of America: Los Angeles's Central Avenue Jazz.* Charleston, S.C.: Arcadia, 2014.

Olesker, Michael. *Front Stoops in the Fifties: Baltimore Legends Come of Age.* Baltimore, Md.: John Hopkins Univ. Press, 2013.

Osborne, Jerry. *Rockin' Records Buyers-Sellers Reference Book and Price Guide, 2010 Edition.* Port Townsend, Wash.: Osborne Enterprises Publishing, 2010.

Palmer, Robert. *Baby, That Was Rock & Roll: The Legendary Leiber and Stoller.* New York: Harcourt Brace Jovanovich, 1978.

Rayno, Don. *Paul Whiteman: Pioneer in American Music.* Vol. 2, *1930–1967.* Lanham, Md.: Scarecrow Press, 2009.

Rhodes, Don. *Say It Loud!: The Life of James Brown, Soul Brother No. 1.* Guilford, Conn.: Globe Pequot Press, 2009.

Rolling Stone. Rolling Stone 500 Greatest Songs of All Time, vol. 1, *1950s–1960s.* Van Nuys, Calif.: Alfred, 2008.

Ross, Sharon Marie, and Louisa Ellen Stein, eds. *Teen Television: Essays on Programming and Fandom.* Jefferson, N.C.: McFarland, 2008.

Rubin, Rachael, and Jeffrey Melnick, eds., *American Popular Music: New Approaches to the 20th Century.* Amherst: Univ. of Massachusetts Press, 2001.

Ruppli, Michel, comp. *The King Labels: A Discography,* vol. 2. Westport, Conn.: Greenwood Press, 1985.

Ruppli, Michel, and Ed Novitsky. *The Mercury Label: The 1956 to 1964 Era.* Westport, Conn.: Greenwood Press, 1993.

Russell, Tony. *The Blues: From Robert Johnson to Robert Cray.* London: Aurum, 1997.

Salem, James M. *The Late Great Johnny Ace and the Transition from R&B to Rock 'n' Roll.* Urbana: Univ. of Chicago Press, 1999.

Samuels, David. "Rhythm and Jews." *Tablet,* June 12, 2016.

Sharp, Steven. "John Brim: The Ice Cream Man." *Living Blues* 118 (December 1994), 39–45.

Shaw, Arnold. *52nd Street: The Street of Jazz.* Boston, Mass.: Da Capo, 1977.

Simmonds, Jeremy. *The Encyclopedia of Dead Rock Stars: Heroin, Handguns, and Ham Sandwiches.* Chicago: Chicago Review Press, 2006.

Smith, R. J. *The Great Black Way: L.A. in the 1940s and the Lost African American Renaissance.* New York: PublicAffairs, 2006.

Spörke, Michael. *Big Mama Thornton: The Life and Music.* Jefferson, N.C.: McFarland, 2014.

Staggs, Sam. *Born to Be Hurt: The Untold Story of Imitation of Life.* New York: St. Martin's, 2009.

Steptoe, Tyina L. *Houston Bound: Culture and Color in a Jim Crow City.* Berkeley: Univ. of California Press, 2015.

Townshend, Charles R. *San Antonio Rose: The Life and Music of Bob Wills.* Urbana: Univ. of Illinois Press, 1976.

Ward, Brian. *Just My Soul Responding: Rhythm and Blues, Black Consciousness, and Race Relations.* London, UK: UCL Press, 1998.

Ward, Ed. *A History of Rock and Roll,* vol. 1. New York: Flatiron Books, 2016.

Weatherford, Mike. *Cult Vegas: The Weirdest! The Wildest! The Swingin'est Town on Earth!* Las Vegas, Nev.: Huntington Press, 2001.

Werner, Craig. *A Change Is Gonna Come: Music, Race and the Soul of America.* Ann Arbor: Univ. of Michigan Press, 2002.

Wertheimer, Alfred. *Elvis '56: In the Beginning.* New York: Macmillan, 1979.

Williamson, Joel. *Elvis Presley: A Southern Life.* New York: Oxford Univ. Press, 2015.

Wynne, Ben. *In Tune: Charley Patton, Jimmie Rodgers and the Roots of American Music.* Baton Rouge: Louisiana State Univ. Press, 2014.

Zak, Albin J., III. *I Don't Sound Like Nobody: Remaking Music in 1950s America.* Ann Arbor: Univ. of Michigan Press, 2012.

Zoglin, Richard. *Elvis in Vegas: How the King Reinvented the Las Vegas Show.* New York: Simon and Schuster, 2019.

Websites

American Blues Scene. "Blue Law: Hound Dog vs. Bear Cat." March 19, 2014. https://www.americanbluesscene.com/blues-law-hound-dog-vs-bear-cat/.

Discogs. "Chuck Higgins and His Mellotones." https://www.discogs.com/artist/3070223-Chuck-Higgins-His-Mellotones.

———. "Jack Turner and his Granger County Gang." https://www.discogs.com/artist/1676181-Jack-Turner-And-His-Granger-County-Gang.

Elvis Australia. "D. J. Fontana, interview with Arjan Deelen." https://www.elvis.com.au/presley/interview-djfontana.shtml.

Sun Records—706 Union Avenue Sessions, March 1, 1953–March 31, 1953. https://www.706unionavenue.nl/83574047.

Index

Note: Page references in *italics* refer to photographs.